Awaken to the Truth

and

Transform Your Emotions into Unconditional Love

Smitha Jagadish

For more information, email:
theschoolforenlightenment@gmail.com

Print ISBN: 978-1-9169074-6-1
Ebook ISBN: 978-1-9169074-7-8

Dedication

This book is dedicated to everyone looking to awaken to the truth and who would like to transform their emotions into unconditional love. If you have been searching for the truth and have been disappointed in the search, this book can help and support you on your spiritual journey. Many of us struggle to overcome our emotions daily, and here in this book are a few suggestions for anyone looking to transform their emotions into unconditional love.

GET YOUR FREE GIFT!

To attain the best experience with this book, readers who download and use *Spiritual Enlightenment* can implement ideas faster and take the next steps needed to *Awaken to the Truth*.

Receive your free copy by emailing the code AWAKEN to the email address below.
www.theschoolforenlightenment.com

In the subject line, enter the phrase **Free Book**.

Table of Contents

Part 1: Awaken to the Truth

Chapter 1

Introduction

What does it mean to awaken? To awaken means to wake up from your daily routine, repetition, mundane work, everyday beliefs, and concrete knowledge. As a spiritual seeker, you will awaken as you read this book.

You've started searching for the truth long before you found this book. But until now, you simply followed the path ahead of you—whether you liked it or not or enjoyed it. You kept doing what you were meant to do, told to do, and what you thought you should do.

But once you awaken, you start to question everything around you. You start to see life differently. It's almost as if you've been living in a dream state, and now you're waking out of it. This is the most basic form of awakening.

As you grow in your spirituality, your levels of awakening will also expand to encompass a bigger reality.

What You Will Learn From this Book

You'll learn to awaken your inner power. If you feel you are living on auto-pilot, are tired of your everyday routine, or are feeling confused, this book will help you awaken to the joy around you.

If you're ready to discover more about life than you currently know or want to wake up to a deeper truth, this book is for you.

You'll discover where you are on this journey of awakening to the truth and what elements might stop you from awakening. You'll discover the hindrances and blockages in your life. And you'll find bridges to cross to help you transform and awaken to your inner power.

You'll learn how to observe everyday life carefully. And you'll discover how to observe the truth, practice the truth, and speak the truth.

The Benefits of this Book

Once you have awakened to the truth, you'll look back and see how much you believed in things that didn't matter. You'll realise how much energy, time, focus, and attention you lost in believing what you thought was the truth.

Once you awaken to the truth, life is free and liberated. You're relaxed. You're more confident. You let go of things easily without taking them to heart. You look at everything and smile joyfully. You allow things—good or bad—pass by you without holding on to them and ruminating about them.

You won't be lost in profound ideas or exhilarating events, but you will be well-balanced. You will live in the moment, aware of everything happening around you. It's a beautiful way to live life.

My Promise to You

After reading this book, I promise you that you will awaken to the truth, loosen your beliefs, and clearly see the world. You'll see life, see love, and see everything around you in a completely different way.

You will have the unique gift of seeing everything before you without being disturbed, just as if you are watching a film. You will not be affected by anything happening around you because you're awakened to the truth. No more false beliefs; no more convoluted ideas or concepts will hold or control you. You will see challenges and let them go.

You will live a relaxed life—knowing the truth, being the truth, and awakening to the truth. You will cherish every moment.

Chapter 2

Awakening

To be awake is to be self-actualised. You're not trying to be someone else or something else. In our everyday lives, trying to be someone, become something, or want something becomes routine. You feel like you're always searching.

This sense of searching arises because you're not yet awake to yourself, your situation, and your everyday life. Unconsciously, you search, want to learn, and desire to become awake. You don't know you're doing this. You think you're living a good life; you're surviving.

But actually, your life's purpose is to awaken. That's why you're living this life. Yet, you've likely never been told this simple truth. Once you become conscious of why you're doing what you're doing and start asking questions—peeling away your unconsciousness—you'll become more aware of what you're doing.

Once you become aware of what you're doing, you'll slowly connect with your awareness and start to awaken.

Being awake is not doing anything else, not becoming something else, not desiring to identify with anything else. Being awake is simply connecting to the essence of you. The core of you. The being within you. You have no external identity. You have no form that needs to change or be better or different. You're simply awake—in a wakeful state.

Awakening Versus Awareness

It's often easy to get confused between awareness and wakefulness. Awareness is being aware of something or yourself. Wakefulness, or being awake, is being awake from your unconsciousness. You can't be awake for something else. You can only be awake within yourself through awareness. We come to wakefulness through awareness. They are connected but not the same.

We must first understand that awareness is a complex state to be in. The good news is many practices are available to help you become more aware.

Here's an example. Consider the sun and its rays. The sun's rays represent the state of awareness. The state of being awake is represented by the sun itself.

The essence of who you are as a being is awakeness. Living your daily life well is supported by awareness. Awareness helps you become awake. Meditation and self-discovery are awareness practices that help you become awake.

Discovering Who You Are Versus Awaking to the Truth

What is the difference between discovering who you are and awakening to the truth? The difference is that you must first discover who you are. In discovering who you are, you will be awakened to the truth.

Discovering who you are is about exploring who you thought you were all your life and then dissolving all the ideas, identities, and thinking patterns of who you thought you were. Letting go of them will reveal who you are.

In contrast, awakening the truth is more universal rather than personal. It is the truth of everything. This truth also encompasses the ideas of what we think truth is—the deeper truth, the universal truth, the ultimate truth that we were told or trained to believe.

Awakening to the truth requires a dissolution of all the beliefs others have told you that you do not yet know within yourself. At the same time, you begin to embrace and embody an awareness of who you are, and as you discover yourself more fully, you will awaken to the truth.

Knowing the Truth Versus Awakening to the Truth

Knowing the truth is dependent on someone else's awakening. Others have discovered various truths; they have sought and explored all their lives and found what was true for themselves. You have learned information from them, which becomes your knowing of the truth. Yet, in this case, you know their perception of the truth, but you haven't discovered it for yourself.

When you come to the truth this way, you haven't actually discovered it. You aren't awakened to the truth. Knowing is almost a second-hand truth. It can become slightly false because as soon as the truth is known to someone and they explain it, you're learning the information second-hand. You have not yet experienced the truth first-hand.

Knowing the truth—as expressed by someone else—can bring you closer to the truth. It can bring you awareness, clarity, and a certain amount of intelligence and open certain doors for you.

But awakening to the truth must be experienced first-hand. You have to do the work and have the experience to experience a complete picture of the truth.

That said, knowing the truth is better than not knowing the truth at all. Knowing the truth helps you come closer to awakening to the truth than you'd be if you walked blindly in the company of the lies that surround you daily. Knowing the truth removes a few clouds that dim your clarity, but knowing the truth is different to awakening to the truth.

Awaken to Your Gifts

We're all born with a gift. The gift of life is for us to grow into, expand into, become aware of, learn about, and master. Once you master this gift, you share it and help others with the same gift. This gift continues to expand outward over generations and civilisations.

It is essential to become aware of your gift. When you were born, you were given this gift for some reason—perhaps to influence the world or your family—yet your attachment and desires may have masked this gift you received at birth. You've lost track of this gift, and you've lost track of the meaning of your life.

Yet only through this gift can you fully live your life. This gift helps you grow as a person as a being and allows you to transform as you create a new life.

Once you reconnect with this gift, live with its presence, and explore it fully, you can share this gift. Then, you will be given another gift to live the next life, and in this way, the gift continues within you towards eternity. This is how you master each and every gift in life.

Become aware of the gift that you have; become aware of the expertise that you have. Become aware of how you can manifest this gift and share it to help others realise their gifts.

So, for example, if you were born with a gift of spirituality and recognise something beautiful in you that helps you see the beauty in others, honour this as your gift. If this is your gift, start to explore it. Become aware of it. Discover and learn things in this context. As you learn, you experiment and stretch yourself. You would then share knowledge about this gift as you meet others with similar gifts.

Even though each gift is individual—unique for each person—the context might be similar. Sharing your gift with others who have similar gifts helps everyone grow. Your gift would remain yours alone, but you can still serve others and express it from your point of view.

In a moment of self-reflection, observe yourself, check in with yourself, and try to uncover the unique gift you were given at birth. You've always had this gift, and you still have it.

Perhaps you've stopped exploring your life through that gift and have become attached to other superficial areas of life, and you might feel you are not fulfilling your purpose. You're not being who you were born to be.

If you're not living actively with your gift, you constantly feel pulled to something, a foundation you always desire to return to. No matter what happens in life, whether you're sad, happy, at ease, or challenged, you continue to be drawn back to your gift because that is where you find the most peace and contentment.

You will be reminded of your foundation, your desire to explore it deepens, and you'll realise that distractions begin to fade away.

Even though life's distractions might seem important, discovering who you are and being who you are is the best way to live your life. Being awake to your gift is about creating a new life once again.

Awaken to Creativity

When you understand and awaken to your gift, you become creative. The gift helps you access the ocean of creativity. If you explore your gift, you will uncover new ideas, new truths, and new thinking. New love comes from this pool of creativity. As you access your creativity, you sometimes feel unsure of your creativity. Why is that?

You may be unsure of your creativity—unsure of bringing your creativity through your gift into this world—because nobody's ever heard of your approach before. Or nobody is yet able to acknowledge what you're creating. Nobody seems to be able to relate to your creativity. This is natural because your expression of your gift comes from a place of newness.

Anything that comes from a place of newness will always be new. And then it can never be understood or compared by anyone else. It is up to you to translate your gift and what it offers. You need to be able to explain it. You need to be able to communicate with people about your truth.

It is your duty to take your gift into the world, to expand the gift, and to share its creativity and beautiful newness with everyone else. It will always be new because it cannot be compared. It can be different, but it cannot be wrong. So, with this truth in mind, take your creativity into the world. You're bringing newness to the planet, and in this way, you awaken your creativity.

Awaken to Euphoria

What does it mean to awaken to euphoria? Most of the time, we are taught to be happy or feel a sense of euphoria by engaging with external stimuli or by attaching ourselves to material objects. Our only perception of euphoria—probably false—is induced by something external that creates this state. The true euphoric state comes from within.

So, how do you reach true euphoria? What causes it to arise? It comes from the effort you put into your growth, self-cultivation, and self-realisation. It comes when you use your gifts, strength, power, and intelligence to express yourself creatively.

You connect with your new awareness and awakeness and create something which hasn't existed before. And with this new creativity, you produce a product, a manifestation. When your creativity is made manifest, it touches people. When you give yourself and your creativity to them—when they buy this product or enjoy your creation—the euphoric state naturally appears.

So you can see how much effort, intelligence, gift, creativity, and love have gone into manifesting euphoria. Now, you can see how the euphoria you encounter in everyday life—the one which has been advertised, taught, or induced—seems false. When you detach yourself from this false, euphoric state created by external sources and turn inward to find your gift, creativity, and innate intelligence, then use this new awareness to create something to help humanity, you will experience endless euphoria. And you created it. No one else. When you awaken to this euphoric state, you will live a beautiful life.

Awaken to the Journey of Life

We're all on a journey to awaken in life. No matter what you do, you're trying to awaken yourself, consciously or unconsciously. You're doing this every minute of your life.

We're all on this journey to summit the mountain of life that we are climbing. On this journey, we will encounter many stumbling blocks, hindrances, attachments, states of happiness, joys, and other dilemmas. We may spend many years or lives there. Or we may be able to detach and awaken from these desires, identities, and concepts and move on and finally, with considerable effort, we may reach the summit and awaken to the truth.

This might be the most beautiful experience of your life, and it might only last a split second. After all your efforts, you might fall right back down the mountain, especially if you get caught in the journey itself and the exhilaration of attaining the summit rather than appreciating the glory of the awakening.

Some people summit mountains solely to tell others of their accomplishments; this becomes another form of attachment. They repeat the journey over and over again—falling off the mountain, climbing the mountain again to awaken to truth momentarily, then falling once more. This cycle prevents them from awakening completely.

If you could awaken to a level where you live on the summit without being pulled down by life's good or bad experiences, you wouldn't need to repeat the journey. You will have awakened for good.

This awakening to the truth is not a split-second experience but creates a new way to live. You live in this awakened state all the time. This is what you're looking to do. When you awaken to truth, you live it every moment of every day.

Awaken to Authenticity

We all feel being authentic is being real—being one's self, being natural, living with ease and flow. This state already exists for you.

However, this notion of authenticity is often misinterpreted or misunderstood. It is often represented as true nature, that no effort is needed to connect with or sustain it. In fact, it's just the opposite.

Authenticity arises through the effort put into attaining it. It's about the purity of it. It's about giving up everything to grow. It represents a will to expand and leave attachments behind. It requires going through a struggle to create, manifest, and blossom.

This work can only be done by you, yourself. No one else is involved. No other input is integrated—not even the slightest of any kind is accepted in true authenticity. It's just you 100 per cent.

Authenticity is not just about being natural or real because you don't even know what that is yet. Your authentic self is a new creation that has not existed before.

Your authentic self is the first of its kind in millions of years. You connect with it consciously by learning, understanding, and working towards it. Connecting with your authenticity requires work, effort, and creativity. It requires struggle, pain, and letting go.

Awaken to Newness

What does awaken to newness mean? Newness is something that hasn't been encountered before. It refers to something that has not yet manifested, which means it is growing, expanding, moving, and flowering. So, awakening to newness means this quality of newness found in all of us that we haven't woken up to yet.

We are used to thinking we know things; if we don't know, we research to find out. We search for answers from outside ourselves and copy other people.

We rarely go within to discover answers, but when we do and learn something we'd never known before, that answer comes from newness. Newness is a new understanding, a new seeing, and a new truth that will fulfil you. In this way, newness adds to more newness.

Newness grows in newness and expands, and you become the creator. Imagine you want to create something new at this moment. You open yourself to the potentiality of this creation and bring that out of you. You manifest it and share this newness with everybody else. In this way, you are complete within yourself.

We often depend on outside materials to help us understand past information, history, forecasts, and the future. In this way, we've lost the creativity within us. We must relocate it.

You must go deep inside yourself and be patient. Aspire to be original and authentic. As you search for answers on the inside, your newness will grow. The more and more you use it, the more you will feel fulfilled and nourished. Your newness will sustain you and help you grow. You're self-sufficient in this newness. You are complete.

Awakening to newness means slowly stopping your dependency on, learning from, and attachment to external influences. You turn your attention and curiosity inward, going deeper inside yourself. You learn patience and perseverance. You are curious, questioning, and discovering. Choosing to turn inward will ignite the newness; you'll recognise it and begin to grow, leading to a new sense of fulfilment.

Awaken the Mother and Father in You

Life is not just about waking up in the morning, going to work, and living a routine. Families with a mom and dad are smaller versions of the bigger universe. As a child, you received love from your mom. No mother wants her child to face difficulties or know hardship; she wants you to discover your potential.

You learn to overcome attachment to your mother and learn the educational nature of the father, who teaches you about the world and shares knowledge of how everything works. You learn knowledge from Dad and bask in love from Mom. Then you go out into the world to realise your true potential, discover who you are, show the world what you are and what you were created for, and use your creative, imaginative, beautiful nature to serve the world.

Engaging the world this way is like your family of origin. The earth is the mother; the sun is the father.

19

Initially, you learn everything from the mother, and when you're ready, you leave those attachments and learn from the father. You live a terrestrial, earthly life, and when you're ready, you move out into the universe to discover who you are and realise the potential you have to serve the universe.

In this way, you see the juxtaposition between the family of origin and the family of the universe. In that sense, you begin to see your tasks or responsibilities at a global or universal level. As you grow, you emerge from the smaller family and enter into a bigger responsibility for the universe.

The best way to describe our lives is as if we're attached to the simple love of our mother and don't want to grow up to move towards the light of our father. You may not feel ready to go through the sun to discover your unlimited potential.

We are meant to remain connected to Mother Earth; she offers us much love. Yet our consciousness calls us to grow; there's so much we don't know. Many of us haven't yet learned anything from Father Sun. Once we learn to leave the attachments of the earth, we're more free to learn about the universal knowledge of the Sun. Once we learn from the Sun, we can extend to the Universe and fully experience our unlimited potential.

Awaken to Manifestation

Manifestation is the materialisation of a thought or an idea already present. To manifest something, you need to know of it. Without knowing, you cannot manifest it. It appears as an image, which is then created so everything we see around us is manifested. Manifestation is knowledge and understanding. It is going deeper, peeling back layers, and getting to know things.

Yet, manifestation is not original. We've seen things and manifested things for aeons, but manifestation is not the truth.

Here's the difference—manifestation is creation. Truth is greater than manifestation. Once you discover the truth, manifestation is just for play, something to create and enjoy.

But without realising the truth, without discovering the truth, without being awakened to the truth, manifestation is all we can see. Thus, it appears as though manifestation is the truth. But manifestation is only a vision. When you arrive at the truth, realise the truth, and are awakened to the truth, then manifestation gains value and becomes useful.

Awaken to Illusion

Illusion tells us that everything is outside of us. We feel that everything we see is separate from us. Notice an object or entity. It is an illusion. Since we see that everything is outside of us, we obviously believe it is not within us, creating separation.

But when you start doing spiritual practices, and as you progress in your spiritual journey, you will begin to realise that nothing is outside of you. Everything is inside of you. When you come to this realisation, you'll realise everything you thought was outside you is just a reflection.

A reflection is always an illusion. A reflection is not the truth, not real. If something is reflected to you, you can not grasp, hold, or embody it. It's not true or real. Because it's not true, where is the reflection coming from?

Now, go to the origin of the reflection. Who sees this reflection, and where is it being reflected? You will notice that the reflection is coming from within you, and it is reflecting outside of you. You have misunderstood the reflection as something else.

When you realise this—through experiencing many disappointments, pain, and suffering—you'll see you've been chasing the reflection and haven't discovered the origin of the truth. You will return to the source of the reflection and realise that the reflection taught you that everything is within you.

Everything you see outside of you right now is within you. Within and without are not separate. Everything is unified, and within the unification is the truth.

Awaken to Freedom

We all aspire to freedom. We're all looking to be free. But can we handle freedom? That is the first question we need to ask ourselves.

What would you do first if you had all the freedom in the world? Ask yourself and see what answers bubble up. Notice if your answers are something like, "I want to spend as much money as I want how I want," or if it's like, "I want to be the most beautiful person on the planet," or "I want to be the richest person on this planet." If you have any of these answers to your question about freedom, you might recognise this isn't quite a mature answer.

Freedom is a great responsibility. That is the first thing we must understand. To make the most of freedom, one must have maturity, personal development, and a will to serve. Freedom empowers and motivates you to grow and expand. As you grow, you help others grow, expand, and become motivated. This growth, expansion, and motivation help make this planet a better place to live in the short term and for future generations.

When your answers to what you'd do with ultimate freedom become altruistic, then freedom comes to you even though you weren't searching or longing for it. Freedom is waiting to fill all of us.

Yet, you may not feel freedom at the moment, and this is because you're not ready for it. Perhaps if it came today, you wouldn't have the self-control, strength, and inner wisdom to use it well.

So, when you ask for freedom, be prepared, cultivated, grown, and mature. Freedom comes to those who are ready—ready to change this world, ready to make this place a better place for future generations. Be ready to serve. Be ready to help; ready to transform everybody on the planet. That is true freedom. It will arrive when you're ready.

So keep preparing. Keep working. Keep trying to better yourself by raising your awareness and becoming awake daily. Put effort into growing, cultivating yourself, learning, loving people, sharing with people and helping them. Then, effortlessly, when you might least expect it, freedom comes to you.

Awaken from Relationships

Why do we put so much emphasis on our partners in our relationships? Why do we have so many expectations about others? Often, we're looking for an ideal partner or the perfect soulmate. But could the perfect partner be ourselves? This is the question we need to ask. Are we looking to have a relationship with ourselves? Is this perfect person, the ideal person, actually us and we are unaware of it?

All the qualities that we're looking for in an ideal partner are the qualities that need to be developed within ourselves. Work toward having the ideal relationship with yourself.

Note all the ideal things you expect from your perfect partner, then look to see if those qualities are within you. If you haven't developed these qualities for yourself, you clearly expect them from someone else. We want to benefit from someone else showering these qualities upon us because we cannot be bothered to develop them within ourselves.

Sometimes, developing excellent qualities within yourself is a difficult task. The effort, maintenance, and growth required to develop ideal qualities is tremendous. However, investing in personal growth is worthwhile. Look within yourself and see where you excel and where you need to grow. Then, develop those underdeveloped characteristics within you. As you grow, your expectation of finding an ideal partner might disappear. In this way, you awaken to the ideal relationship—the one hidden within you.

Awaken to Teachings

Growing up, you may have encountered many excellent teachers who have shared insightful ideas and thoughts. Many leaders, mentors, spiritual teachers, and gurus share their knowledge with the world.

Why do we like to follow them? And how do we follow them—blindly or consciously? We often follow teachers because we don't know how to live by ourselves. We think someone else will pull us out of our misery, suffering, or bad behaviour. We want someone else to put in the effort instead of expecting ourselves to do the hard work of becoming better humans.

That is why some go to ashrams and meditation centres to follow gurus and teachers and listen to them. We want someone to tell us how to behave. We want someone to tell us that we are doing wrong. We want someone to guide us in the right direction.

And why is that? Life seems so simple, but yet we make it complicated. Why do we not know for ourselves what is good and what is not good, what is excellent behaviour and what is not to be done? Life is filled with seemingly simple things like love, compassion, and knowledge.

Intelligence is born in every single human being. But we are lazy. We don't want to expend effort to better ourselves. We don't want to work hard. It is often comfortable to stay where we are without evaluating whether we are in a good place or not a good place. We do not want to invest the effort into transforming ourselves. But why is that?

This is the question we need to ask ourselves. Why aren't we motivated to grow and become the best human we can be? To be a human being who shares love, compassion, and help? To be a human being who wants to help themselves and all others have a better life?

Do we want somebody to tell us we are bad, evil, or lazy and that we can't get over our own attachments? Is that so? I don't think so—not for everyone.

Awaken to your own teachings. Awaken to listening to yourself. Awaken to trust that you will do the right thing, are a good person, and wish no evil on anyone. Choose to develop these qualities by constant self-observation, meditation, and love for oneself and others.

Is this possible? Can you do this yourself without relying on someone else to tell you how to be a good human being? Yes. It is time to awaken to your inner wisdom and teachings.

Awaken to Maturity

All of us have different explanations of maturity. But the most suitable definition is "someone responsible". Someone who has taken responsibility personally. Not just at an intellectual level but in a deeper way of taking action, creating change, and creating transformation.

Maturity is not just about observation, seeing, and understanding. It has a depth of understanding and growth, which leads to further actions. Witnessing and observing life is the first step, but you see results when you go deeper into observation. It comes with a sense of responsibility.

Moving beyond superficial observation leads to a transformation. That transformation is the effort you make to actualise maturity. This transformation is not just within you but is also expressed outwardly. Maturity embodies the responsibility of action and creates movement, change, and revolution in and around you.

With maturity comes responsibility. When you're mature, you don't think someone else will sort things out for you or take care of you or that everything happens by itself. Becoming mature transcends this kind of thinking.

When people are not yet awake, they often ignore things or think they can get away with doing whatever they want because somehow everything else will be sorted. But how are things sorted? Who is doing the sorting?

The mature person is the one sorting the problems. The immature person continues to create the problems. Choose to embrace maturity. Be the one who steps up and sorts things out. Create positive transformation.

It requires effort. It takes responsibility. When you're ready to transform yourself and others, then you belong to the family of mature people.

The Purpose of Spirituality

Spirituality helps you realise everything you experience in your life is your own creation derived from your own behaviour. That is the truth. Spirituality helps you understand who you are in daily life as you interact with yourself and others and learn how to become a mature human being.

Without spirituality, you don't care who you are or how you behave. You are immature. But when you step into spirituality, you become an adult. You realise you've had enough of being childish, behaving erratically, and being unconscious. You're ready to grow into adulthood.

So, what does it mean to be an adult? It means you have awoken from your dream. You move beyond your life's small desires that try to satisfy the mind. You step away from a constant wanting of something you don't have. Releasing the grasp helps you step into adulthood and develops your maturity.

This realisation of embracing adulthood—looking to grow as a human being—is what spirituality is about. You're taking responsibility for yourself, for everyone else around you, and also for this planet. Your maturity and spirituality, internally and externally, affect the bigger universe. You become a citizen of the planet Earth, a citizen of the universe and its solar systems and galaxies.

You have decided to take that first step into growth. You've moved beyond wanting to be a baby, toddler, or innocent child unaware of who you are. Your childlike self wants to enjoy the trees, plants, toys, and everything around you without looking after them and being unconcerned about destroying things. Stepping into adulthood goes hand in hand with awakening your spirituality.

The Universal System

The universal system is very similar to our family system. But everything is on a larger scale. For example, think about a child in a family. He could have a mother, father, siblings, aunts and uncles. It is the elder's responsibility to raise the child and help him understand who he is as a person. They teach him to develop good values, be helpful to parents and relatives, and be a good citizen, family member, and community member.

This structure develops the child and is infused with love. In the same way, the parents are also children of the mother and father of the earth. The earth is like a big system, and the mother and father of the earth need to teach their children how to behave—how to take care of the planet and the people around them and be good citizens who help the earth grow to the next level.

In the same way, you can also be a family member of the solar system. Imagine there are parents of the solar system. Those parents are looking after you and teaching you. You are a child of the solar system and learn how to be a good steward of the earth and the solar system. It expands outward. You are not only a child of your parents and the earth; you are a child of the solar system, the galaxy, the universe, and the multiverse. The expansion and your role within it is endless.

You are not just growing up or maturing from being a child to an adult in your family or individual life. You are maturing into something larger. With this in mind, cultivate your personal growth beautifully, for you are a child of all of creation itself. This growth and development expand your consciousness, and you become a child of the universe, taking responsibility and helping others to grow, change, and transform as you did.

Awaken to Transformation

What does it mean to transform? As a simple example, imagine a child reluctant to share her toys with others. She grasps her toy tightly. It is valuable to her; it is her world. Her entire day revolves around this toy—it is her favourite, and she loves it infinitely. It is almost as if this toy has become a part of her.

If you try to take this toy away from her, she cries. She is upset and angry. She would try anything to get this toy back or to keep it.

In the same way, some adults become deeply upset when an object or individual they love is taken away. They are so upset they almost give up on life. They become hopeless. Sometimes, the sadness is so great that it lasts for years. Relationships, jobs, and wealth may be lost. In this instance, the person is behaving like a child.

For the child, if her toy is lost or taken away, she becomes sad or angry. But as an adult, many toys are available. You understand that many experiences create your life—jobs, relationships, material things—they are each just one aspect of the breadth of life's journey.

As you grow, you will experience many things. You have an opportunity to understand and learn. You eventually can detach from losses and upsets better than the child can when the toy is removed. The child's world is small; she doesn't yet know what will come and how she will mature and become stronger and more capable. But you, as an adult, see the broader horizon.

As an adult, you have learned from your childhood experiences and developed into a better human being. What you once lived through helps you grow wiser. These experiences were for your development. The more you can digest these experiences, move on, and take lessons from them, the more you can grow into an open-hearted individual, helping planet Earth and expanding yourself to the universal level of experiences. In this way, you transform into a larger human being.

Awaken to Unlimited Potential

When you reach a point of unlimited potential, you are writing a new story for your life. You are the creator of your life, and in actuality, you are starting from scratch. You are intelligent, open, clever, bright, aware, awake, loving, kind, compassionate, and caring.

You've accomplished much up until this point, but you're ready to begin the next phase of your life. This is a beautiful place to be, and it feels almost unexplainable because until now, you had ideas and were trying to achieve something, get somewhere, accomplish something, and succeed. Yet, due to life's push and pull, you could not reach a point of creation.

This point of unlimited potential is where creation manifests. You are literally at the point of creating something new and never seen before. This is an immense responsibility. It is where you write, draw, paint, and create in whatever form inspires you the most beautiful, loving, caring, affectionate, compassionate life for yourself in this universe. And this new life is yours to enjoy from this point onwards.

If you'd like to learn more about this process, please explore my online course *Awakening to the Truth,* https://bit.ly/3QHfk5m.

Chapter 3:

Levels of Awakening

Awakening has multiple levels and happens in stages throughout life as you progress on your journey through discovering the truth. During your journey of spirituality, you will have several awakenings. Personally, I have experienced eight awakenings, and I explain them in this chapter as levels one through eight. Let's begin with an overview:

- **Level 1:** Awakening from suffering. It is the first time you realise that you are suffering and can do something about it.
- **Level 2:** Awakening from our desires. You have had hundreds, if not millions, of desires. From the moment you're born, desires layer on top of one another, and you now realise you wish to wake up and detach from these desires.
- **Level 3:** Awakening from the world. Until now, you believed you lived in the world and did not see it as separate from you, and now you realise that you are

yourself and can differentiate your life from how you live in the world.

- **Level 4:** Awakening from your beliefs. From infancy, you've had a belief system constructed by input from outside sources, including family, friends, education, work, and community. You now begin to see the beauty in following your internal wisdom rather than blindly following the input from others.
- **Level 5:** Awakening from energies. In life, you have not yet recognised the difference between self and energy. This level helps you slip out of the push and pull of various energies.
- **Level 6:** Awakening from unconsciousness. Now you've awakened to suffering, desires, external beliefs, and energies, you realise all of this lives in unconsciousness, and you're ready to explore unconsciousness more deeply.
- **Level 7:** Awakening to self. When you understand unconsciousness, you're ready to explore your self and will learn about the aspects of self and awaken fully to it.
- **Level 8:** Awakening to the truth. Once you've awakened these levels, you question the truth itself. What is the truth? Who constructed this truth? What is the real truth? Once you've awakened all these levels and begin questioning the truth, you awaken to your inner power.

Awaken to the Truth & Transform Your Emotions Into Unconditional Love

For most of your life, you balance between multiple worlds of existence. One world is materialistic and hierarchical. A second world is filled with energy from galaxies and embodies truth.

A third world is a non-existence, a complete nothingness; it contains no material, belief systems, truth, or life—a total contrast between existence and non-existence.

If you can awaken to both worlds of existence and understand the relationship between existence and non-existence, you can live a beautiful life. When you awaken to one and not the other, or you haven't realised each, you'll experience heaviness, problems, and suffering.

Your goal is to transcend them all. The first step is to awaken to both worlds of existence and live in harmony, peace, and understanding of both worlds. One isn't better or more appealing than the other; one isn't worse or less valuable than the other.

Awakening helps you understand the relationship between them, the harmony between them, how one cannot exist without the other, and how they are both equally important and relevant in your life. Having that deeper understanding in every moment and enjoying them both as reflections of each other is the ultimate realisation of existence and non-existence.

Level 1: Awakening from Suffering

What is suffering? It has many interpretations and meanings. What one person perceives as suffering, someone else may not. One person might think a challenge is okay and manageable, and someone else might find it nearly impossible to deal with. For some, suffering is almost inevitable; they're caught in it all the time.

How can you awaken from what you consider to be suffering? How do you overcome it? Consider the idea that when you, the person, feel caught in suffering, you can choose to change your perception. Notice your thinking and ask yourself why you feel stuck in the suffering. What factors around you or within you are causing the suffering? Why are you in this place at this time?

These observations—these questions—will help you recognise your beliefs, attachments, and desires. As you explore these elements, you may begin to understand the root of your suffering more deeply.

Alternatively, your suffering may be related to something else completely. For example, if your child is hurt, you suffer along with her. Or if your friend is having trouble at work, you suffer along with him. This suffering is caused by attachments to expectations. Things didn't follow the predicted plans, and you suffer when your loved one doesn't get the desired result.

Suffering arises from many reasons, but underlying all of it is attachment. When you awaken to subconscious expectations, you begin to better deal with unexpected results. When you learn to release expectations, your suffering begins to decrease. You awaken from the attachments that keep you in a dream world.

You begin to awaken when you realise attachments, desires, and expectations are the root of your suffering, and you choose to let them go. You're conscious. This realisation leads you to an awakening from suffering.

Level 2: Awakening from Desires

The realisation of suffering is the first step to waking. Most of the time, you don't know you're suffering. This realisation and subsequent awakening help you find a way to escape it.

When you discover that your attachments and dependence on expectations cause suffering, you can enter level two, awakening from desires. Again, you are likely unconscious of your many—perhaps several lifetimes of—desires and constantly desire one thing after another. These desires are a continuous stream, replacing one after the other to satisfy yourself to the point where you are no longer aware of your never-ending desires. We think this is all our life is about.

You fulfil yourself with something. Then the next thing pops up. You work hard to fulfil the second desire, then a third desire pops up and then you work extra hard to fulfil that desire. Then another pops up, and so on. In this way, you have multiple desires seemingly without end.

When you realise this string of desires has no end—hundreds of desires catch you and pull you down—you may feel defeated. You see the cycle with no end in sight. However, by noticing and observing this pattern, you begin awakening from desires and no longer waste your time and energy trying to fulfil your desires through external means.

As you awaken to this desire cycle and begin to observe how desires pull you down rather than lift you up, you will begin to distance yourself from your desires.

For example, if you have worked toward creating a healthy, fit body yet still feel dissatisfied, it is time to move into the realm of the mind. Or, if you have love, health, and financial stability yet are still dissatisfied, it's time to move into the realm of living rather than accumulating.

What often happens when we are at a certain level, either body, mind, love, or life, we tend to stay stuck at that level, moving horizontally rather than moving vertically upward. To grow and awaken to the truth, you want to evolve upward.

For example, suppose you're in the level of love; you're searching for more love, more relationships, and more connection with family and community. All you seek is love. In that case, you're expanding sideways and moving horizontally rather than moving upward to the level of life. To grow, you need to explore life, you need to find out about life, and you need to discover life. That's the next level for you to discover. Growing upward prevents boredom, frustration, and disheartenment.

The same is true if you're wealthy. For some, if wealth is unlimited, they may get bored, wonder what to do with their time, and get into trouble. Rather than travel horizontally and become bored, travel vertically and move to the next level.

Awakening from desires means observing the layer where you live most of your life. Identify where you are, then see if you're overdoing something. If you are, then reduce that behaviour and put that energy into moving upwards. Expanding horizontally is merely repetition and doesn't require much effort. It's just obsession. If you find you're obsessed with or addicted to something, it may be because you're stuck at one level.

To learn more about moving between body, mind, love, life, light, and energy synthesis levels, please refer to my book *Discover Who You Are* or my online course https://bit.ly/3Y21sEL.

Level 3: Awakening from the World

To awaken from the world, we first need to understand that the world consists of human-made definitions, creations, and perspectives of living in family, community, and society comfortably and enjoyably. We live in the world. We are influenced by the world. Yet, we don't know the difference between the world and reality. We eventually accept our perceptions of the world as reality and begin to be influenced by and absorbed in it.

Awakening from the world means realising a bigger reality exists beyond the human-made world and being willing to connect with that greater reality.

Level 4: Awakening from Beliefs

A belief is assuming a truth that you have not personally experienced. You might have heard or read about this truth but have not yet discovered it for yourself.

Beliefs are common; they're a way of navigating the world and new experiences. However, as we accumulate more and more beliefs, we can become confused, as one belief says one thing and another belief says something else. These beliefs often prevent us from discovering the truth for ourselves.

For example, you read in an article that the sun radiates a certain amount of heat. You believe that information because you haven't discovered it for yourself, and the scientists espousing it say it's a fact. You take this fact seriously; you adopt it as your belief.

In this way, your whole life is filled with beliefs. Since you haven't discovered it for yourself, you don't fully know the truth about it. Only when you see the truth for yourself—experiencing it directly for the first time—does the belief take on a new meaning. It becomes a truth rather than a belief and stays with you forever, deeply inside you.

Awakening from beliefs means discovering more direct truths and weaning yourself off external information from others. Discovering truths for yourself enriches your life and contributes to a life of authentic truth.

Level 5: Awakening from Energies

Energies are in a state of constant movement—pulling and pushing up and down, in and out. In this constant motion, you cannot discover who you are because you always move from one thing to another. When caught up in the movement of your body's energies, emotions, thoughts, and desires, you cannot rest in peace. The energies constantly run from one end to another. It's excitement. It's frustration. It's anger, agitation, and anxiety.

Awakening from your energies means discovering and observing the individual energies you experience. Distinguishing between various energies helps you observe without engaging in them. If you observe these energies carefully and master them, you will awaken and reduce the likelihood of being carried away by them. As you awaken from chaotic energies, you achieve greater levels of peace and calm.

Level 6: Awakening from Unconsciousness

Unconsciousness essentially is being a lost state of not knowing who you are. In this unconscious state, it becomes easy to assume everything you see around you is true, yet you also feel a tremendous amount of confusion. You have wants and needs and are consistently drawn toward chaotic energy.

Most of us are lost in our unconsciousness. It's a dreamy state. It is a state devoid of reality. It is the state we're looking for. You feel at home. It offers comfort, love, affection, and the essence of belonging and being wanted. This unconscious state draws us increasingly into the sleepiness of not allowing us to remember who we are.

We think everything is beautiful and everything is okay. It's a state of floating, wandering, seeking, searching, and being lost. It keeps us tangled in memories and attachments. We often go to work in this state of unconsciousness without knowing who we are. We sit with our families. We talk to our friends and neighbours. We go on holidays. We go dancing, we party, we eat. We tend to live most of our lives in this unconsciousness, believing it is reality.

Awakening from unconsciousness helps you discover who you truly are. You begin to see more clearly your truth and the reality of your life.

Level 7: Awakening to Self

The self is your spiritual being. It is present from the moment of birth. As you grow, you begin to see yourself in something. That first, pure, authentic awareness of self is often connected to your spiritual self.

Often, identity is derived from attachment to something. For example, if you have loved to watch and play sports since childhood and you associate yourself with sports, it becomes part of your identity. It is almost as if you become the sport and see the world through sport. Your first identification with sports happened when you were very young, and you didn't know anything else. You didn't have any perception of yourself outside of sports. You observed sports, played sports, and took it into your being. You felt a deep attraction, which became the foundation of who you are.

You begin to identify with other things as you age, but this first identification always stays with you. Yet, as you begin to identify with other things, confusion arises. You forget you are the sport, and you begin to lose yourself.

Once you realise you are lost, you can trace a route back to your foundation, that authentic pure you that is your spiritual being from birth. As you reconnect with

your spiritual self, you realise you are more than sport—
it is not you; you are not it.

So, spirituality is a self-discovery tool through which
you discover your real self. It is more than an
identification with something external. It is the mirror
that helps you realise who you are.

On top of this spiritual self, many other selves have
emerged from attachments to external things and
experiences. But when you choose to explore inwardly,
you will arrive at the spiritual self, and once you arrive at
your spiritual self, you awaken to who you truly are.

Another way to describe this is to imagine yourself as
the earth, with a big circular mirror surrounding you. All
you see in the mirror is the sky and earth, including the
mountains, rivers, plants, animals, human beings, and
everything else. If you were the earth and seeing yourself
in the reflection, you would think everything you see is
outside of you. The trees, flowers, humans, animals, and
mountains are seen in the mirror but don't seem like you.
It takes you, Earth, a long time to realise that everything
you see in the mirror is actually yourself—grown by you,
developed by you, given birth by you.

Imagine assuming that everything you see in the
reflection is something outside yourself. You see the
reflection in the mirror and want to hug, hold, touch, and
smell it. After many losses, disappointments, pain, and
suffering, it takes you a very long time to realise you can

not touch the reflection. What you see in the mirror can never be felt.

Then, one day, after several disappointments, you realise that what you see in the reflection is really within yourself. All of that is a part of you. You can't feel what is in the reflection, yet you can feel yourself. You are the thing represented in the reflection.

This is the realisation of the truth. This is the realisation of the self. Now, rather than imagining yourself as the earth, simply be you. Imagine looking in the mirror. All the glory you see reflected in the mirror is within yourself. You no longer need to feel the disappointment and pain of not touching and embracing the mirror; you can embrace yourself. Everything you see in the reflection is actually inside of you. When you understand this, you are awakening to self.

Level 8: Awakening to Truth

Awakening to the truth is awakening to the realisation of the nothingness of unlimited potentiality. It is the ability to create a new being.

Before bringing this beautiful expansion into your life, your ideas and emotions were constricted. You were told to remain small in consciousness and being.

But now, as you awaken to truth, you can open up to limitlessness. No one can constrict you after you've made this realisation. No other past memories or external influences can force you to be smaller than your unlimited potential, a state of creative abundance. You begin living your life every moment in this boundlessness, which is the truth. Staying in this boundlessness is what awakening to the truth is all about.

Imagine the life you're born into is a big mountain. Your goal is to ascend to the mountaintop. Others—who have reached the top of their mountain—tell you that you will see the truth at the summit. They tell you it's beautiful, incredible, and a blessing and offer other flowery descriptions.

But you have not yet started the journey. You imagine this summit based on the words of others. You have a belief based on what you hear. And with these ideas from others, you begin to ascend. You live your life. You climb this mountain every day. Little by little, you discover things along your journey. Sometimes you get lost. Sometimes, you get stuck because of attachments— perhaps because a spot is beautiful or you think a place is too hard to climb. Your climb is filled with stops and starts, distractions, and diversions.

If you have the will to continue climbing and begin shedding the tales you've heard from others, you'll finally reach the top. This happens only with the support of love, determination, effort, intelligence, and creativity. You have cultivated all those qualities during your journey. You attain the summit, and what do you see? What do you discover? What awakens within you?

Awaken to the Truth & Transform Your Emotions
Into Unconditional Love

You are awakened to your attachments—the blockages, suffering, misery, joy, and happiness—and have left them behind. You awaken to pure truth, a new space, new seeing. Once you reach this place, you create a new life. You are now in charge of everything.

The real truth about the truth is that "there is no truth". What does that mean? It means, first of all, we are surrounded by lies. Others tell us what life is, what love is, and what the body is. You absorb all this information from other people. You begin to believe some things quite deeply, sometimes to the point where you think what you hear from others is the best thing for you and that it is true. You may even spend your entire life following a belief, and then when the belief is shaken by some accident, misfortune, or unpleasant incident, you begin to question it.

You question the validity of the truth. How did this truth come about? Why did I believe in it? What's really true now? When your core beliefs are shaken, and you lose trust in that belief and start to question it, you begin to question all your other beliefs.

When most of your beliefs are shaken, disbelieved, and discarded, you end up with fewer or no beliefs. At that point, you start to discover the real truths in your life. You discover truths for yourself and are not bound to information someone else provides.

When most of your core beliefs and the truth you believed are shaken, you come to a point where you no longer have beliefs. You no longer believe in truths espoused by others. When you realise this, you suddenly have unlimited freedom. Imagine the potential you'll have when nothing is stopping you. You can create your own truth from a place of freedom. You become responsible for everything that happens from this day forward.

You are now awakened to the truth. Truth is what you discover. In this discovery, you are creating and expressing the truth. You are beginning anew. After you awaken to the truth, you will begin explaining and teaching people how to approach the truth. Yet you are only telling your way.

Teach others how to find the truth, and remember it may not look like your way.

As you awaken to the truth, you naturally become a responsible human being—a human being who's discovered the truth and knows how to behave on this planet and engage with others in a loving, compassionate, kind, and truthful manner. It is as simple as that.

Yet awakening to the truth sometimes takes lifetimes to attain. Why does it sometimes take millions of years to realise and actualise being a true human being? Is it because we resist change? Or do we resist the effort required to be loving and kind? Why aren't we naturally good human beings, and why do we put so much effort and work into striving to arrive at simply being good?

Awaken to the Truth & Transform Your Emotions Into Unconditional Love

It's because of our unconsciousness. We are often unaware of how we live in each moment. We don't observe ourselves. We don't observe others. We don't realise how we speak, what we speak, how we behave, how we interact, how we think, how we feel, how we move, and our actions towards ourselves and others.

Awakening to ourselves—the way we are, the way we conduct ourselves—is the real realisation. Without this, we would be sleeping forever. It's as simple as that. Wake up and become aware of how you behave, interact, and what kind of human you are in every moment. Don't let anyone else tell you how to behave. You are an adult and mature. You might have children. You may be a teacher. Learn about yourself, awaken to your truth, and then help others do the same.

Being a good human seems to be complicated. Why have we allowed this to happen? How can we help others when we ourselves don't know how to be truthful? Start with yourself. Observe and love yourself and everyone else. It's as simple as that.

Chapter 4

Practices to Help You Awaken

You can read more about these practices in the book *Spiritual Enlightenment: The Intelligent Way to Awaken, Enlighten, Discover Your True Self, and Find Liberation.*

Power Flow Practice

Power Flow Practice helps you completely relax and let go of all the tension in your body. Any stress you might have accumulated or any worries over time can be dissolved through this practice. Any longings, any emotions, any addictions you might have can all be reduced and eventually eliminated.

Power Flow Practice helps you settle your busy mind and encourages your body to relax. By slowing your mind, you can learn to tap into the unlimited energy available to us all. We all have access to this infinite power source, which may lie dormant and undiscovered.

Power is unconditioned pure energy, the energy that has not been here before and has a quality of newness. This power is potential energy and helps us more clearly see reality.

Power Flow Practice is a remarkably simple but effective strategy that can be mastered by anyone. You can start anytime, and you don't need any special tools. Continuous practice of this technique will take you to higher levels of accomplishment in your life.

The benefits of this practice are life-changing, and the effects are instantaneous. Learning to access the purest potential energy has many benefits, including creativity, clarity of mind, positivity, high energy, increased mental strength, and better sleep quality.

Through this practice, you'll slowly learn to relax your mind, stop your mind, and then come out of your mind eventually. You can see the effect of it within three weeks, and you'll move through the phases of awakening, enlightenment, discovering your true self, and finally finding liberation. This is a one-stop practice for everything.

Power Flow Practice is best done in a quiet place. A quiet room is helpful as, initially, noisiness can interrupt this form of practice. You can also light a candle if it helps you to create a calm and serene surrounding. You can play calming music to relax and let go of your body.

Awaken to the Truth & Transform Your Emotions Into Unconditional Love

Lie down and take a break from everything. When you lie down, close your eyes, take a couple of deep breaths, and intentionally stay awake. There's no need to worry about breathing in any particular way, focusing on the third eye, or anything else you may have read about in other practices.

You are completely relaxing—you allow your body to let go, your mind to slow down, your emotions to be what they are, and your awareness to be free. There's no restriction, no focusing, no concentrating. You're being rather than doing.

Start with just five minutes a day and add a bit more time daily. If you can, try to do this practice each day at the same time and in the same surroundings; it will slowly make it easier for your body and mind to settle into that state quickly.

When you lie down and intentionally stay awake, you will notice sensations start to rise from your feet; the sensations begin to gather and eventually will rise to the crown of your head.

Everything happens by itself; you don't need to think, label, or understand anything. If you feel like nothing is happening, that's okay. Just stay with the practice of lying still and remaining awake.

You'll slowly notice the sensations in your legs start to rise, and you slowly begin to feel the sensations in your hands, chest, shoulders, and neck until they concentrate near your forehead. This process clears all the tension and stress built up in your body that has moved up into your head.

As you continue, you'll notice that all your body's accumulated tension eventually feels forced into your forehead. If you find this sensation uncomfortable, just continue breathing; the discomfort will pass. Slowly, you will feel that this force rises above you and moves upwards.

When this force rises above your physical body, it's as though somebody's taken away all the tiredness, stress, and tension, bundled it all up and thrown it above you. The body is relaxed, and you have recovered your body from any strain or tension at this point.

Eventually, you will start to see your thoughts clearly once your bodily sensations have died down. Often, thoughts begin to take the place of physical sensations. You are now entering the mind.

Once your bodily sensations fade and you enter the mind, you'll notice your thoughts. They can be short thoughts or long thoughts; they can be old or new. Again, there is no need to do anything. Let the thoughts come and go; you don't need to observe anything at all. You need to stay awake; that's all you must do.

When you enter the mind, you often feel you have no direction. No one stands with a signpost saying this is where you need to go, or this is where you need to turn left or right. Free yourself from expectation, and allow your instinct to take over. When you were born, you relied on instinct; you automatically knew to search for your mother's breast for food and void your waste. Eventually, over time, you learned how to crawl, walk, speak, write, read, and develop intentional thought. It took practice and trial and error.

Taking care of your mind through Power Flow Practice is like learning the next level of thinking. By releasing intentional or negative thoughts, we create space for intuitive, enlightened ideas to enter. We exercise our bodies to stay healthy; this practice is an exercise for our bodies and brains.

By staying awake, you consciously overcome your body's sensations and disturb the mind's thought patterns. By staying awake and simply being without thinking, you enter a pure awareness of yourself. You are not engaging your bodily, emotional, or mental needs. This practice helps you face your everyday life through expanded awareness. This increased awareness allows you to deal with life situations with a sense of clarity, peace, and calm.

This practice also helps you to detach from life's events. Emotional detachment doesn't mean that you no longer care; rather, you can view events from a place of peace and clear-headedness. As you become skilled with this practice, eventually, you'll find that no matter what comes your way, you'll be able to face it calmly and find that solutions arise nearly without effort.

Power Flow Practice helps you reduce confusion in all aspects of life. Where you've been twisted emotionally begins to unwind. Solutions to problems become clearer. You start making effective decisions and start seeing life as it is rather than through your veil of emotional or physical responses and temptations. This power you develop is the real power to overcome anything in life.

As you continue this practice daily, you will experience a sense of focused energy in your forehead. As the energy rises above your body, you'll start seeing a light.

Initially, this light appears faintly, seemingly at a distance. However, as you practice this meditation, slowly building from five minutes to ten minutes to fifteen and on to twenty and more as the weeks and years progress, you will come across a bright white light.

This light arrives after the many thoughts in your mind cease. You'll notice this white light seems as though it's flowing over you. It clears all your physical pain and all your mental stress. It cleanses you of your built-up emotional struggles and eases your physical pain.

Eventually, with continued practice, you'll float through this white light, going higher and higher, until you discover your heart has been opened. You connect through your heart rather than your mind. This becomes a place where you know you can empty your body's tension, where your emotional and mental stresses dissolve, and where your entire system becomes clean and renewed. You will eventually master to hold your breath to an optimum level by being able to tame the life force in you.

As you clear your accumulated stress and tension over time, you can detach yourself from the unconsciousness. Unconsciousness being the old you. You will discover a new consciousness. When new consciousness meets your breath of life, you transform into a New Being. This Being will expand and rise above to be liberated in life.

Empty Through Living Practice

In this Empty Through Living Practice, you will learn how to awaken from unhealthy or excessive physical attachments, ranging from a flavour you'd like to taste, a workout plan you'd like to follow, a soothing sensation you can't live without, to deep desires and addictions.

You'll learn how to end bodily entanglements and minimise the amount of control your body has over your day-to-day life. This practice will help you bring your deep desires to the surface and understand what drives them. You'll begin to free your body as if emptying it from these desires.

Over the years, you might have accumulated many physical desires to the point where your body feels like it can no longer breathe. This Empty Through Living Practice helps you to wake from your unconscious and unaware state to a conscious life in this body.

As I deepened my Empty Through Living Practice over the months and years, I noticed a clarity in my life. All my doubts, issues, and troubles slowly ebbed away. As I cleared one layer of self-doubt, another layer revealed itself. Layer after layer rose to the surface until I began to discover my deepest self.

As self-doubt rose to the surface in waves and layers, I realised that other desires and attachments rose up as well. I had deep attachments to many things and ultimately had to deal with them.

I discovered that the easiest way to deal with most of my deepest desires was to embody them and live them. I chose not to hold myself back. I chose to embrace and experience all the desires and wishes that bubbled up. However, I consciously experienced these events with acute awareness.

For example, when I fancied having a nice meal out, I'd book myself a table and invite a friend to join me; sometimes, I'd even eat a wonderful dinner on my own. If I felt like going to the gym, I would go; if I felt like spending an afternoon on the couch watching movies, I would. If I felt like learning something, I'd study.

In this way, big or small, I consciously and with awareness lived out most of my desires.

As you start completing your desires, intentionally savouring each moment, everything underneath starts to surface. The reason we have so many desires is because we haven't consciously lived them. Once they are lived consciously, they will slowly disappear.

Hence, the Empty Through Living Practice will clear your desires one by one and lead you to a more conscious life.

Through this practice, you stop accumulating inconsequential desires. As you practice experiencing events and daily life with awareness, you begin to live a more complete life. Everything becomes satisfying, and you move away from the dissatisfaction of wishing for something but not making it happen.

You learn how to detach. Detachment arises when you live out an experience with awareness. Attachment occurs when you wish for something to happen but cannot bring it into reality.

As you practice living with awareness and create experiences for your desires, you add fewer unfulfilled desires. You begin to live out your oldest and deepest desires intentionally and become Empty Through Living.

Do your best to minimise your need for control over the outcome. Remember to live your life and find peace within yourself. As you enjoy your life and begin exploring these deeper desires, you'll see that what you always wanted to do, what you always longed for, is within your grasp. Do your best to experience the world; go out and live your existing desires in the safest way possible.

When you make this choice, you minimise the nagging thoughts constantly echoing in your head. Taking action on your desires ultimately leads to detachment from them. Your mind is no longer filled with daydreams.

Remaining stuck in a daydreaming cycle is why your desires and longings are not fulfilled. All you're doing is imagining it; you're not taking action. Turning these daydreams into lived events is the best way to empty yourself and keep yourself new, uncluttered, and fresh all the time.

Through this Empty Through Living Practice, you discover how to live your life by letting go of your physical attachments towards your deep desires, past memories, and unfulfilled actions. You only have to experience everything once consciously, and then the hunger for the same experience subsides.

An unlived life with an accumulation of desires may cause you to become numb and desensitised to your reality. Emotional responses to imagined life experiences keep you bonded to them. Emotional attachment—either positive or negative emotions—blinds you from seeing the reality of life.

This Empty Through Living Practice can be done anytime and anywhere. Its benefits include overcoming unpleasant habits, addictions, abuse of self and others, and freeing you from being burdened by heavy emotions. In effect, the Empty Through Living Practice may help you feel unattached, grounded, relaxed, and free.

The Essence of Questioning Practice

In this Essence of Questioning Practice, you teach your mind to question everything. You will attempt to avoid taking for granted all you've been taught, what you've observed or read. As if with an innocent mind, you will question your beliefs and years of unverified thinking.

This practice encourages you to question everything. You reach deeply into your roots and the darkest corners of your mind and heart and pull everything into the light.

If you're angry, you question why you are angry. If you behave a certain way, you explore what caused you to behave like that. You reflect on what factors were involved. You wonder, "Who is this person acting in this fashion? Am I acting from my true self or as guided by the teachings of someone else?"

If you're happy, are you happy because somebody else would be happy in such a situation? Or are you genuinely delighted because we see the beauty before you?

The Essence of Questioning Practice teaches your mind to question everything rather than accept anything blindly. It teaches you not to simply follow something just because it appears good, enjoyable, or happy.

As my meditation practice evolved and grew, I worked with the Power Flow Practice and the Empty Through Living Practice. I continuously attempted to pursue detachment and began to unload years of accumulated mental, emotional, and physical baggage.

While intentionally living these two practices, I added a new element. I started to question my every action.

Before this awakening, most of my actions were unconscious, involuntary, and reactive. If you take a clear look at your life, you'll notice most of your actions are not conscious; it's almost like your actions are reactions to other responses.

It seems as if we've been trained from a very young age to behave in certain ways. We're taught when situation A arises, reaction B is the appropriate response. We begin to develop routines and abandon variation.

When I was juggling a job, raising two kids, and managing many other life requirements, I easily fell into unconscious routines. I was exhausted, and the thoughtless patterns made it easier to make it through each day. Sometimes, I'd think about switching things up, but I couldn't seem to enact change. I then felt guilty for wanting to create any new life patterns, so I gave up and fell back into the rut.

Your mind will tell you that you haven't done enough, are not good enough, haven't reached your capacity, and still have so much more to do. Your mind asks, "Why isn't that finished? Why isn't this finished? Why is that project incomplete?"

Your mind and its routines begin to take on a form of authority and control; it's like working for a narcissist.

You almost feel bullied by all the tasks your mind wants you to do. Often, it asks too much.

To appease the mind, you become so used to your routines that you cannot live without them. I had a strict daily routine that I followed for many years. If I didn't follow it, or if one part of it was out of place, I would panic. I would feel unsettled and would be convinced that something in the day would go wrong. My mindset and outlook for the day were corrupted.

Perhaps you have routines like this. You may do everything possible to keep this routine going. Whether it makes sense or not, whether we have enough time for this routine or not, we've been told that the mind needs routine.

Somehow, you feel your day has to follow this consistent path to ensure your lives are more at ease.

However, often, we don't question why we follow this routine. Rarely do we ask, "What happens if I don't do this? Am I such a robot that all these actions must take place for me to maintain a positive mindset?"

Have you ever questioned your old routines? Have you ever wondered why you get up on one side of the bed every day or why you eat a particular breakfast daily? Have you ever questioned why you wear certain clothes or go to the gym consistently? These routines don't seem to have any connection, yet in reality, we've adopted them, and our unconscious mind has taken control.

We've not cultivated the ability to question ourselves and our habits. We simply follow the patterns the mind has built for us over the years. The mind seems to have taken over our free will and tells us what should be done or not done. We will go the extra length, the extra mile, to please the mind.

The Essence of Questioning Practice helps you overcome these routines. It enables you to expand beyond your current limitations. You develop the strength to ask your mind, "Why do I have to do this? Why does it have to be done this way?"

This questioning of every action helps you develop a certain intelligence, which is useful in seeing the truth rather than simply reacting as if on autopilot.

In this practice, you question yourself deeply. You intentionally reflect on all of your thoughts and actions. This, in turn, leads to deeper insights. Ultimately, this practice helps you see the truth and evaluate your judgements, beliefs, and opinions more clearly.

You don't notice it, but your mind rarely tells you you're doing well, that you've done enough, that it's time to rest. Instead, your mind continually asks you to do more.

However, once you learn to meditate and learn to Empty Through Living, you have more energy, clarity, and awareness, so you can see your actions objectively.

In the Essence of Questioning Practice, you ask yourself, "Why am I doing all this cleaning? Who's actually going to judge whether or not the kitchen is spotless? Who will tell me the shelves are not dusted perfectly?"

In some cases, you may diet nearly until you die, but who are you trying to please? In other cases, you may try to accomplish fifteen tasks before you rest for the night when, in reality, doing seven today and the rest tomorrow may be good enough.

The Essence of Questioning Practice helps you recognise that you can free yourself from self-judgement. By questioning the very root of a problem, you will become closer to your true nature and discover new intelligence.

As you gain more and more awareness and clarity, you begin to question each of your actions. This questioning allows the bubbling up of a remarkable form of intelligence.

This intelligence that arises through questioning your actions is the truth. It is the real truth that allows you to see that your circumstances are not as you imagined them to be. Instead, you begin to see the reality of life without the filters of old patterns. You see the real truth of life.

As more and more wise intelligence arises from your questioning, you begin to observe your life's essential truth.

This Essence of Questioning practice can be done anytime and anywhere. It is particularly useful for busy people as it does not require a special place or time to carry it out. You will benefit immensely from overcoming many of your self-imposed restrictions in life.

The benefits of this practice include deconditioning years of unverified knowledge and patterns from your mind, deeper insight, personal freedom, a clearer understanding of life's nuances, increased wisdom, and higher intelligence.

Observing the Truth Practice

The Observing the Truth Practice is done when you've finished questioning everything and start seeing the truth for yourself rather than taking anything for granted.

Now that you've worked with The Essence of Questioning Practice, you're ready for the Observing the Truth Practice. To observe the truth, you must detach from the trappings of the mind.

The mind is a maze of thoughts, beliefs, dogmas, and wrong-thinking. Only through observing what is happening to you and around you can you discover the truth. Only then can you come out of that mind-maze and walk toward enlightenment.

When you question everything, you will hear an intelligence providing answers. This intuitive intelligence speaks to you from the depths of its wisdom and reveals the truth. This practice takes patience. Be kind to yourself in the process.

Awaken to the Truth & Transform Your Emotions Into Unconditional Love

Begin moving away from the reliance on books or other information resources to answer your questions. Instead, spend time sitting quietly with yourself. True knowledge is gained through observation and through listening to your inner self.

For example, if you want to learn about a tree, rather than find a book about it, spend time loving it and observing it. Look closely at the tree and notice its movements, its colour, and the smell of the bark. Imagine talking with the tree and observing its intelligence in its reactions and communication with you. This is real learning about someone or something in the present moment. This is an example of Observing the Truth Practice.

You're learning for yourself from scratch and not relying on input from others. This is your first-hand truth through experience. The Observing the Truth Practice does not apply solely to learning about the physical world. It can be used for mental, emotional, and spiritual learning as well.

Let's look at another example. Imagine a situation where someone has emotionally hurt you. Do your best to recall the circumstances accurately so you can observe wisely. Imagine your daughter calling you and saying, "Mom, I hate you." Observe what's just happened.

Normally, we react immediately based on whatever we've learned or been taught in our life. Sometimes, that prevents us from seeing the real truth of the matter.

Instead, observe your pain without reacting. Explore why you feel this pain. Is it because you are overly attached to your daughter, perhaps emotionally dependent on her for love and attention?

If this is the case, and you see it when you follow the Observing the Truth Practice, you recognise this sense of being emotionally hurt is inevitable. However, you also realise you are emotionally attached and can begin working to detach yourself from her emotionally.

From this new perspective, when you continue to observe your reactions during your conversation with her, you begin to see how emotionally heavy your attachment to her had been, and now you begin to feel lighter.

You used to feel emotionally controlled by her words, expressions of feelings, actions, gestures, and so on. But by observing the truth of the situation, you're learning about yourself and your learning about your relationship with her.

Here's another example. If you respond in a particular way when your husband comes home, old patterns cause this behaviour. The next time he comes home, observe your thoughts and how your body reacts. Notice how you hold yourself and respond to his words and presence.

You might be emotionally attached to particular ideas of him, or you might have a certain image of him in your head but without knowing that you react a certain way. The Observing the Truth Practice helps you begin to see and express yourself clearly, honestly, and truthfully as you let him know what you truly feel and think. By observing the truth and speaking the truth, you start to learn to live in truth, which, in turn, expands your reality.

This practice replaces rumination—constantly thinking about thoughts not based on fact—or denying how you feel. This practice helps you examine your emotions and release emotional baggage. When you don't speak your truth, your emotional layers become heavier and heavier, eventually wearing you down.

As you continue with the Observing the Truth Practice, you begin to see things more clearly, and you can more effectively create positive and healthy changes in your life.

Observing the Truth is an effective and uplifting method for dealing with emotions. We begin to see the hidden things we normally gloss over because we're emotionally enmeshed.

Observing the truth takes practice. Because we are so caught up in our emotional distress, we often have difficulty seeing what is happening in stressful situations. The Observing the Truth Practice helps you create and maintain a gap between the situation—or the people involved in the situation—and you. Distancing yourself and observing what is happening in front of you offers a tremendous sense of internal wisdom.

This gap is the birth of awareness. This distance and detachment allow us to glimpse reality. As you slowly develop this gap and create space between everything in life, you will enter a detached reality: awareness.

This awareness is pure seeing; it's not the seeing of the mind or the reaction of emotions. It is simple, natural, peaceful, clear awareness. This awareness can grow and extend to the level where you will eventually start to live in this state. Observing the truth at all times becomes second nature. When you live in awareness, you can handle any situations which come your way. Your heart opens, and you soften, becoming more compassionate toward yourself and others.

As you enter this awareness and open your eyes, you'll be able to see others without judgement. You'll be able to connect more easily and peacefully with others. You'll discover your true capacity to give and receive love when you open your heart.

This Observing the Truth Practice can be lived every moment of the day. With patient practice, you can observe the truth and maintain this distance between yourself and situations. You'll learn to live with detachment and an open heart, both of which help you evolve emotionally and discover your true self. You will develop the art of living with intuitive intelligence.

Though this is an advanced practice and particularly useful to someone already on the path to finding their true self, it is worth the effort. Ultimately, this practice helps you develop self-awareness and cultivates inner peace, a feeling of connectedness, deep love, and a greater sense of ease and wholeness.

Mirror of Consciousness Practice

Consciousness is the source of all-seeing. The Mirror of Consciousness practice is advanced and facilitates opening to a new consciousness. In this practice, you connect with objective reality, and your mind becomes still. When the mind is still, consciousness enters into you. When consciousness starts to enter, you find a state of bliss.

In this Mirror of Consciousness practice, you will teach your heart to love your mind and teach your mind to admire your heart. The core of the practice remains closely connected to yourself. You're not looking outward with the heart and mind; you're looking inward. This practice brings the mind and heart together, and each uses the other like a mirror of consciousness.

Typically, we observe the outside world, yet even that observation is partial. We've been trained to look outside and learn from a young age. Rarely are we encouraged to look inward. Most of the time, we're taught that self-observation means only seeing the body.

Yet often, what we observe around us, outside of ourselves, doesn't make any sense. It's like watching a movie without a direct and personal relationship with you.

We identify what we see outside us, but we don't know what exactly is going on. We see people argue, strive ambitiously, love, and hate. From a young age, we've observed our parents and our family react and behave in certain ways, and we somehow assume what we see is the right way to learn or do things.

Where is the self-seeing in all of this? The movie continues—and will continue forever—until you choose to recognise that it is simply a movie and not real. At that moment of awareness, you begin to see yourself and identify that the movie isn't your reality.

But waking up from this movie can be difficult. In the movie, you identify with various roles—mother, father, brother, sister, friend, whatever jobs you've held or titles the world gives you because of the family you were born into. As you wake up, you might struggle to determine where you fit in. You begin to create your own new life every second.

When you're awakened, you see the world's reality for the first time. You start to admire the true beauty of life. When you're caught up in the movie, you cannot see real life; you see only the movie's noisy and confusing world.

At first, learning who you are without playing a role takes time. As you continue learning more and more about yourself, you'll minimise external influences. You'll learn how to feel safe and strong standing on your own. You become confident with who you are.

Awaken to the Truth & Transform Your Emotions Into Unconditional Love

Once you wake up, you will actually see a beautiful life with trees, mountains, and sunshine. You'll recognise that people are more than labels or roles. When this awakening expands, you begin to detach from the fiction of the movie. You become a human being rather than remain a role; over time, you embrace your uniqueness, your independent thought. You walk down the path of enlightenment.

As you learn to be more and more comfortable within yourself and grow into a bigger being, you will start to see that the love and admiration that you craved from the outside world is not what is most valuable. You learn that *you* loving your own heart and mind is most important. This is the foundation of the Mirror of Consciousness practice.

Each day, you strengthen your awareness that you are enough. You permit yourself to love your mind more than anyone else can. You embrace your heart with a tenderness that no one else will offer. As you freely give yourself to yourself, you evolve into a new being. You have connected deeply with your true self. You have connected with the most essential part of you that is at the same time greater than your physical body and mind.

The Mirror of Consciousness practice comes when you live each moment admiring your mind and loving your heart. You no longer need someone else to tell you how good you are. You already know it from the core of your being. You have become whole, unified.

In the past, you've loved someone and gotten hurt, or you've felt dissatisfied with the love you received from your mother, father, family or friends. But now that you've learned the Mirror of Consciousness practice, you realise everything you treasured has been within you all along.

When your true mind becomes aware of your true heart, and when your true heart becomes aware of your true mind, they become still. They mirror one another. When these aspects of your true self embrace one another, they unite, creating a new consciousness. As the Mirror of Consciousness reflects back and forth, it is as if multiple dimensions come into being. You become a new universe born from the union of love and light.

The stillness of the mind converges to a single point before it starts to fall into itself and finally dissolve. As you deepen your self-awareness and self-appreciation, you watch the mind evolve into the root of silence. This silence exists beyond the mind. This silence expands and reaches a state of tranquillity. This silence is the totality of everything. All that there is!

This Mirror of Consciousness practice is effective and simple and can be done anywhere at any time. Through this practice, you will learn to experience a still mind, bloom in bliss, and live in a state of ecstasy.

Freeing of Consciousness Practice

In this advanced Freeing of Consciousness practice, you develop compassion. You learn how to independently follow your path towards discovering your purpose in life. You learn to merge the light of consciousness with the breath of your being. When your consciousness and breath harmonise, they rise above your crown and rest at the top of your head.

By expanding your love and consciousness, you discover your true self and your true passions and start to establish your unique purpose in life. Through this practice, you'll cultivate compassion and learn to share this compassion, through your unique purpose, with the rest of humanity. You will work towards bettering the human race.

As you more thoroughly understand your life's purpose and act on it, and the more completely you embody compassion for self and others, you deepen your connection with divine consciousness. Through this practice, you dissolve your individual self and expand to harmonise with universal consciousness.

Through the Mirror of Consciousness practice, you realise that when your heart loves your mind, and your mind admires your heart, a pure and true love arises between them. This true love gives rise to a new consciousness and a new being. This new being, the true essence of you, has never been on this planet before. It has travelled a long path from unconsciousness to consciousness.

Once, you lived in dim consciousness. You did not know who or what you were. You were sleepwalking through life, not knowing anything and letting things happen to you. Through the Mirror of Consciousness practice, your unconscious becomes conscious, and you become a new individual. This new individual, this new being, is the embodiment of compassion, ready for the Freeing of Consciousness practice.

Who is this new being who embodies compassion? All humans have the capacity for compassion; however, many are still asleep. They have not intentionally awakened their consciousness. They are caught up in the old patterns of their emotions and mind. They're stuck watching the movie of life, not yet able to see the truth.

This compassion is pure love, unconditional love from the union of the heart and the mind. This pure love comes only through new beings. These new beings, of any age, are the ones walking the path of enlightenment. These new compassionate beings help others learn to realise their true selves.

When embodying the Freeing of Consciousness practice, the pure love of your mind and heart flows unconditionally—not only for yourself but also outward like a river into the ocean of being, helping buoy others along the path.

Awaken to the Truth & Transform Your Emotions Into Unconditional Love

The compassion that evolves out of this practice gives rise to a purpose. This purpose is to help others realise their true selves and unleash everyone from the pain and suffering borne from their entanglements and attachments.

As helping others becomes your true purpose, you start spreading love to everyone. You begin to help whomever you find. You help everyone you encounter to realise who they truly are, and you help lift them out of this world of suffering.

This manifestation of love happens not only in this world; it also occurs universally. We connect to universal consciousness. In this way, we build a beautiful mind and heart within ourselves; we help create a beautiful world on earth. Eventually, we expand our compassion and love of truth outward and connect to the captivating universe.

This realisation of your true purpose comes through discovering your true self. Discovery manifests in different ways for different people. You do not create nor manifest your true purpose intellectually. Your awareness of your purpose comes to you or is realised after discovering your true self.

Once you discover your true purpose, you begin to help humanity develop into better beings. You do this with kindness, affection, and love. As you help others, you also expand.

When you expand your true self by sharing your love and compassion with everyone around you, you soon cannot stay within this body. You'll start to rise above. As the union of heart and mind creates a union with consciousness and breath, the union of light and life rises above and extends out of the body through the crown.

At this stage, and moving onward, the sense of heaviness in our suffering bodies lightens, and we harmonise with the divine consciousness—the universal existence itself.

The Freeing of Consciousness practice helps us journey from unconsciousness to consciousness to become one with existence itself. You're one with life, one with light. You flow freely wherever this lightness takes you; you feel no resistance to life or light. You're one with the universe.

The Freedom from Consciousness practice is very advanced and is only suitable for someone who has mastered the Mirror of Consciousness technique. This practice is for someone who has been on a spiritual journey for a while and is looking to complete their journey by attaining liberation.

Your sense of individuality, existence, and consciousness are now freed. The benefits of this practice are that consciousness is now moved out of the body and stays at the crown, leaving you in a state of completion and compassion. A sense of wholeness and freedom arises. Consciousness now functions from the crown of your being. You experience peace and joyful silence! This is liberation!

Part 2: Transform Your Emotions into Unconditional Love

Chapter 5

Introduction to Transformation

Welcome to *Transform Your Emotions into Unconditional Love*. I'm Smitha Jagadish, your spiritual coach, and I want to share a bit about myself in relation to the topic of this section of the book.

Personally, I have found emotions difficult to manage in my life, and I've seen many others struggle with emotions. I grew up in India, surrounded by poverty. I witnessed the effect on people's lives caused by wealth, caste, religion, and education. All of these variances caused people to build internal emotions, and few people were taught how to process them.

We learned to talk about emotions—to complain about them. But the knowledge of processing emotion passed us by. All the unprocessed emotions building up inside have led to a national health crisis because unmanaged emotions affect bodies and minds.

In my spiritual exploration and with my spiritual background and experiences, I learned an open-hearted and open-minded approach to working with emotions. I have discovered techniques and practices that have helped me overcome my emotions and indulge in unconditional love.

Currently, I live in a place of unconditional love, and I see how beautiful it is. And it has taken me a long journey to reach this point. It's taken many years to tackle blockages, problems, and pitfalls on the way to living an open-hearted life. Through this book, I aspire to support you as you learn some of the methods I developed and created. Test them out and see if they work for you. Hopefully, they will help you arrive at the unconditional love of your heart.

Benefits of Reading This Book

This book teaches a simple method for overcoming emotions and discovering unconditional love. It offers practical steps for gaining trust, confidence, and faith in yourself and the universe, and it is filled with helpful practices and meditations that can be used at any time in everyday life. I directly share insights I've had on my spiritual journey and offer authentic explanations.

A primary benefit of this book is that you can begin to identify your various emotions and learn to detach from them. You will learn to use several methods, techniques, and meditation practices which can help you free yourself from attachments, gain confidence, and believe in yourself. Doing these practices regularly will help you understand the meaning of faith, what part it plays in your life, and how it empowers you to free yourself to become part of the bigger universe.

You will learn how to open your heart and enjoy unconditional love. You will live in that joyful place and no longer be ruled by conflicting emotions. You will transform your life and live with unlimited potential.

Who is this book for?

You're in the right place if you lean toward being emotional and have difficulty overcoming those emotions. All humans have emotions, but for some, managing them is more challenging than for others. Emotions play a big part in our lives; sometimes, they're cumbersome. Throughout the years, I've tried various methods to manage my emotions, and I understand what it is like to feel stuck and helpless and need support and guidance. In tough moments, having someone offer you a hand on your journey is helpful.

This book will help you transform chaotic and uncomfortable emotions into unconditional love. It offers an easy-to-follow step-by-step guide to understanding your emotions, the complexities of your emotions, and the layers of your emotional behaviours.

You'll learn to ease out of your emotions by using specific techniques and methods, then follow up with daily practices.

You'll recognise the attachments you have in daily life which cause emotions. You'll identify these attachments and subsequent emotions, pinpointing them and then moving on to the next phase of moving forward. As you evolve beyond attachments, you'll develop a deeper trust in yourself and the universe. You'll cultivate a relationship between the two.

Finally, you'll arrive at a state of unconditional love. You'll embody and live from it, embracing the joy of everyday life.

Chapter 6

What Are Emotions?

Step 1-Recognise the emotions
- Negative emotions: Ego,Cravings, Negative talks,Addictions,Obsessions,Needs,Feeling high, Anger, Frustration, Jealousy, Envy, Hate, Spiteful etc
- Positive emotion: Love,Like,Want,Pleasure,Excitement,Connection,Competitiveness etc

Step 2- Recognise the attachments that cause your emotions
- Self-attachments: Body image, To one's dream, fame, popularity,One's vision,One's goal or ambition,One's feelings,One's experience etc
- Attachment to others: To one's family and friends,To material comforts,to social status,To accumulation of wealth,To partner,To others' ideas etc

Step 3-Beginning the work
- To detach from the self: Power flow Practice,Observing the truth practice,Open heart meditation,Quantum jump mediation,Listening to the heart meditation
- To detach from others: Work on your passion, mirror of conciousness practice, freeing of conciounesss practice,Develop the quality you don't have,Restructure your life

Step 4-Trust and faith
- Trust one's inner voice :Learn to listen to oneself,Manifest your own thoughts,Keep moving forward in life,Speak, love and share your insights,Believe in your capability and potentiality
- Build faith in the universe: Do your part of action leave the rest to the universe to take care of,Remember to stay in alignment with your mind and the universe ,Practice taking the actions from the bigger you.

Step 5- Unconditional love
- Live from your heart,Serve from your heart,Speak from your heart,Follow your heart,Stay balanced in life,Listen to your heart

Overcoming Emotions

How does it all begin? It seems that when we are children, we are free and living in complete bliss. We are unconscious of emotional pain, distress, or unpleasant feelings. The first thing we likely experience is physical pain; we deal with it in our own way and move on. But if someone tells us we are unworthy, bad, disrespectful, spoiled, or whatever it might be, we experience emotional pain.

We try to understand it. But sometimes, we don't know how to process what has happened or try to change it without success; we take that emotional pain into our hearts. Sometimes, emotional pain comes from observing someone else who cannot process emotions themselves, and they stagnate in their heart.

The accumulation of unpleasant feelings in our hearts builds an emotional mountain. It doesn't matter where or how the first pain began. Nor does it matter where we are now. The first thing we must do is recognise that emotions are feelings. You literally feel emotion in your body. Emotions are not mental constructs. You cannot resolve emotional distress by thinking about it.

Feelings in our bodies are centred in our hearts. Uncomfortable feelings are often difficult to deal with, and we wait for time to heal our pain. Time is a great healer. But keeping emotions wrapped in pain and suffering and waiting for them to heal by themselves over time may not be the best plan.

So what do you do? I have discovered the way to release these emotions is to have faith and trust in yourself. If, while growing up, you didn't learn to have faith in yourself and put all your emotional baggage into a corner expecting it to resolve itself, you haven't actually dealt with any of that past emotion.

From Emotions to Unconditional Love

If you haven't processed old emotions, they'll keep coming up. Meanwhile, you haven't learned any new skills for dealing with them, so you keep sweeping them under the rug. Old emotions could be arising in the present moment. Or new emotions could be piling into your heart, perhaps becoming too much to bear.

You feel unhappy, not in bliss. So, you search for happiness and bliss in your external environment. You move out of yourself and rely on others to give you love and feed you joy and affection.

However, the reality is that no one can give you the love you need during your life's journey. You must find it within yourself. No other individual can provide you with bliss. Bliss is a total experience of oneself. It comes with the purity of your heart when your heart is washed clean of chaotic emotions.

So, how do you purify your heart? How do you clear stuck and stagnant emotions? You can empty your heart by connecting with the universe—your bigger self—by letting those old emotions flow into the universe. Put your emotional burden onto the universe.

We all know we exist as the universe. We are the product of the universe, and we are the miniature version of the universe, living in this body as a smaller experience. The universe is intelligent enough to look after every single one of us and more.

Once you see and embrace the intelligence of this universe, you can trust that the emotions you extend to the universe can be soothed and processed, which feels way better than holding onto them in your painful, constricted heart.

When you hold on to worries and take responsibility for the emotions of others around you, you don't realise the weight of these accumulated emotions. You're no longer free. Have faith that the universe will support you.

For example, if you're worried about your children, spouse, parents, money, health, career, or future, notice how much emotional baggage resides in your heart. This worry is a huge responsibility you carry every single day.

With this weight, you cannot experience bliss. You cannot experience the purity of your heart. Once you learn to trust the universe with your problems and trust the bigger intelligence, you become lighter and freer.

Allow your worries to be handled by the universe; you don't have to carry the weight or find solutions alone.

Whether your emotional challenges are your own or you're carrying emotional weight for someone else, universal intelligence will support you. It looks after everyone. All it takes is a leap of faith and trust. You can grow and allow everything to fall behind, set your emotions free, and move forward. Then, you will feel liberation from emotions. This freedom from your emotions and attachment to the emotions of others leads to a state of bliss. This bliss is unconditional love arising from a pure heart.

What Are Emotions?

Love and emotions are two sides of the same coin. We often enjoy love but discard difficult emotions. Emotions are the negative side, and love is the positive side. We often experience or spend more time on the negative side as we learn to pass through the realm of emotions.

As you become more aware and conscious of yourself, you move towards love. When you reach a state where love is always present, you begin to release negative emotional attachments. Once you learn to love all your negative emotions, you reach a stable positive state and begin to naturally release your pent-up emotions. When you attain that level of stability and have developed a good relationship with everything you once found challenging, you begin to step back. It's easier to step back from things when you come from a place of love rather than from attachment and negativity. You willingly let things go. You're converting negative into positive and entering the realm of unconditional love.

Recognising Emotions in Self and Others

Once you understand that emotions are of two types—positive and negative—consider the idea that negative emotions are like cravings. Positive emotions are more of love, but love is still a form of attachment.

Your next step is to observe yourself daily and become aware of how you are caught up in positive and negative emotions. Write down whatever you notice as you begin paying attention to your emotions. Try to spend half an hour writing whatever comes to mind. As you develop this habit of observing your emotions, you can start checking in with yourself multiple times during the day. You'll begin to see whether you are in the throes of positive or negative emotions. At the end of the day, reflect on what you've noticed and written.

Observe the effect of your positive and negative emotions on your day. How or what does a negative emotion make you feel? And what is your reaction to this feeling? For example, imagine you are upset about something, prompting unwelcome feelings. Notice your response to those unpleasant feelings. If you are upset, what would you do? Would you try to forget about it or mask the pain you experience in response to this feeling? If so, notice the effect of your reaction to the negative emotion. Observation of your emotions, your reactions, and the patterns you repeat is essential to learning how to process and release stuck and stagnant emotions.

Emotional Patterns

Once you start seeing that emotions affect your daily life, consider whether the emotion is positive or negative. That's the first step in understanding your patterns.

Imagine a positive emotion being love, which sometimes manifests as wanting. It feels more pleasant than negative emotions. The attachment that comes from love may look like this: I love to have ice cream, I love to eat cake, I love to go on a holiday, I love certain kinds of people, I love these clothes, and so on. Observe yourself as you listen to these kinds of words coming from your mind.

On the opposite side are negative emotions, which may manifest as: I'm feeling sorry, I'm worried, I am agitated, or I am anxious. Or negative emotions may arise as need: I need this person, I need this object, I need this food, or I need this drink. These emotions pull at you or feel like cravings. They create attractions where you lose your consciousness or control of yourself. Most of our work as we grow revolves around these negative emotions.

Observe your patterns of needs and wants; both are forms of attachment. Daily, note your observations, and the patterns will become clearer. Notice what causes your emotions, what you're attached to, and your reactions. Become aware of how these needs and wants occupy your time and keep you stuck in a look of emotional leakage.

Once you start to see your emotional patterns, consciously take actions to move away from them, substituting them with positive responses or emotions. Slowly remove your attachment-driven clinging to needs and wants with newly found awareness, and develop a stronger love for yourself. Cultivate a detachment from external needs and begin to recognise that you can fill those needs and wants from within. As you deepen your awareness of your emotional patterns and work toward finding internal fulfilment, you will move closer to unconditional love.

Trusting Yourself and the Universe

Before you trust the universe, you must trust yourself. If you tend to collect and hold onto emotions because you don't know how to process them or how to react, you will fill your heart with heaviness. Negative emotions accumulate within you because you don't know what to do with them.

Awaken to the Truth & Transform Your Emotions Into Unconditional Love

Eventually, you will learn to trust yourself to know that you can resolve, get through, or overcome emotional challenges on your own, and you learn to trust the universe to solve and take care of the challenges. Having trust in yourself and the universe is the key. In reality, they're one and the same.

You are the smaller version of the universe. The universe is the bigger version of you. Having that relationship between yourself and the universe, having that love between you and the universe, comes from trust. Trust needs to be cultivated between yourself and the big you—the universe.

How do you cultivate this trust, this faith in yourself and in the universe, and in between both? Begin by asking yourself right now, *Do I trust myself? Am I able to deal with any emotions that arise?* Notice the responses that bubble up.

If you feel afraid that your life will fall apart if anything happens, or you're living in fear of emotions, believing that you'll be on a roller coaster of ups and downs if something unfortunate happens, it means you do not yet trust yourself that you're emotionally reliant on other people. When you rely on others to provide love, support, attention, and affection, you won't know how to help yourself if your world turns upside down. You wouldn't know how to face life. You wouldn't know how to grow yourself. This is a common fear for people with emotional issues.

Perhaps you live in constant fear of not knowing how to face the world—face life. Know that even with this fear, you can begin relaxing yourself and learn slowly, step by step, to build trust in yourself. You are able to look after yourself. You are able to free yourself from attachment to others.

The first step is to consider the people who kindle emotion within you and ask why that person stirs your emotions. Are you emotionally connected because you depend on that person to keep you alive? Is it almost equivalent to your breath, where you subconsciously perceive the other person provides your oxygen? Have you attached yourself to others you subconsciously perceive are providing you with a life force you can not access because your heart is frozen with stagnant emotion?

So, how do you solve this? An easy and effective step is keeping a diary where you write down all the emotions you experience daily. What emotional situations do you face? As you habitually track your emotions, you will begin to come to terms with what causes your emotions. You'll see your triggers. You'll see your patterns.

Once you observe patterns and triggers throughout your days, you may begin to see how emotions were possibly transferred from your parents, relatives, or friends. Once you begin to see the origin of your emotions and your emotional connections, you can see more clearly the people with whom you have an emotional attachment. Gaining clarity around this makes connecting more deeply with your emotions easier.

So, you've now written about your emotions and their triggers daily, and you've written the names of the people who lead you to your emotional ups and downs; the next step is to slowly become less reliant on the people who create emotional turmoil within you.

Begin observing your interactions with people that spark negative emotions within you. Ask yourself why you feel so emotional around or attached to these people. What prevents you from staying away? Observe your reliance on these people. Write down your observations. Doing so will help you better understand why you feel what you feel and will begin to offer insight into what you can do about it.

The Conscious Way

The third step above was discovering the people you are emotionally connected to and reliant on and beginning to withdraw your attention and dependency from these people. But how do you do this? It is a conscious process. This consciousness and intentional separation is the fourth step.

Begin this process with a person you do not significantly rely on. Look at your list of all the people you are emotionally attached to and find someone you're attached to and reliant on but where you get a certain amount of enjoyment from this emotional attachment. Begin to interact with this person more consciously.

Notice how you rely on this person and observe what this person provides to you that you feel you don't possess yourself. Once you gain clarity around this, you'll realise what you feel with this person is not so much an emotion as a dependence. For example, if you rely on someone who is into music, and you personally don't have the time for this passion, love, or knowledge of music, your emotional attachment to this person fills that gap within you. Hence, you rely on that person to help you connect to music.

Deepening your awareness of emotions, triggers, and reliances helps you identify the actual idea behind your attachment. You can choose to develop yourself, making a conscious effort to learn for yourself what you rely on the other person for. This ultimately leads to detachment because now you have developed this quality within yourself.

In this way, you're now consciously filling the gaps you previously bridged via emotional attachments with various people. Your conscious cultivation begins to fill emotional gaps for yourself. You will become self-reliant and self-dependent and start to trust yourself more deeply.

When you have identified your emotional attachments and the gaps that require them and begin to cultivate areas of your life that connect with the gaps, you evolve. You become confident. Once you develop this self-trust, you will see how this trust helps you connect with your bigger universal self. This bigger, universal version of you can handle all of your emotions and the emotions of everyone on the earth.

Once you develop trust within yourself and trust with the universe, you are in partnership and oneness. Forever more. You can release all your attachments and dependency on other people and things and put it behind you. Permit the universe to resolve the remaining emotions. Once you trust the universe and have faith it will help you with your attachments, you are liberated from the emotional roller coaster. You become free. You step into bliss, which is the unconditional love of the universe.

Complete Freedom

Life isn't all about the body, even though it plays an important role. From a young age, you've been aware of your body. Perhaps it seems to have taken over your life as you grew up. You had to learn how it functioned. You recognised its strengths and weaknesses. You learned how to feel and navigate emotions.

Perhaps you felt like you had few emotions, all of which were challenging, and you became lost in the ocean of emotion. You tried to overcome, escape, or run away from your emotions, not knowing where they began or ended.

Then you are exposed to love, and you think loving others and caring about them is the source of affection. You become lost in love and think it is the most important thing in life. You believe everybody should love everyone; the earth will be this beautiful place filled with endless love.

You don't yet understand that this version of love is an illusion. You're caught in the illusion, and then suddenly, it shatters, and you realise life isn't all about love. Yes, love exists. Kindness, compassion, non-judgement, and loving another without criticism simply because they're alive exist. This extension of affection is normal.

You think it is extraordinary because you haven't realised the truth of unconditional love. You think what you perceive as love is everything in life, and everyone should have it. However, love is only one aspect of life. It is beautiful and nice—when used in the right context, in the right way.

And then you are exposed to light, to spirituality. It feels wonderful, yet it isn't everything in life. Life isn't solely spirituality. Spirituality is only one part of life. It's part of this whole inquiry of discovering who runs the whole show—who is at the top of the tree in this entire universe. Many people call it God regardless of religion or spiritual leaning.

Awaken to the Truth & Transform Your Emotions
Into Unconditional Love

We are exposed to many things in life, and each takes over our life for a moment. You begin to believe life is all there is and nothing else matters. Just being out travelling and experiencing this beautiful earth is what we think life is. Yet, so much more is available to us if we look for it and are hungry for knowledge. Sometimes, the hunger for knowledge—for information about the planet, humanity, and spirituality—can be all-consuming. Yet you can never have all the knowledge because life and the universe are new every moment, constantly evolving.

So, what is life all about? What are we doing? Where are we lost in all of these contexts? What have we been exposed to in life? Where are we heading? Where are we going? This confusion leads to discontentment. The antidote comes when you believe in something. Clarity comes when you no longer wait for someone to rescue you or fill you up. Confusion dissipates when you no longer try to immerse yourself in love, God, peace, or whatever else you seek. The seeking itself is a distraction and a diversion. It is a way to stay busy, occupied, and obsessed.

Dissatisfaction comes when you think having a perfect body will fulfil you; you work towards it, attain it, and then see it is nothing. It was an illusion that someone else presented to you; some external influence you were attached to suggested you should work toward it. Yet, in the long run, it is meaningless.

This is true for every idea planted in your head by someone else. Realise this. Realise that whatever you're chasing comes from emotional attachments, and each new indulgence is just a phase, a discovery.

The real truth is that no truth exists. This is hard to digest after spending so much of your time and energy, sacrificing so much to get to this point. All that work to realise the truth only to discover there is no truth.

What does that mean? You've just climbed this huge mountain of life filled with struggles. It's like climbing Mount Everest and reaching the top and seeing nothingness. There's no expansive view, no other people, no guide, and no authority. No one is in control of all of creation. No one is in control of your life or anybody else's life. There's no head of state, no prince, princess, king or queen. You don't even feel God. What happens now? What is the next step? Where do you go from here? Does it mean you can do anything you want because no one tells you what you can or can't do? What happens when it doesn't matter what you do and everything's okay?

From my perspective, this means that the only things in existence are physical elements and universal laws. And we have no control over either. Whether you're standing on the mountaintop or not, it doesn't matter to the elements and laws. They just do what they are meant to do. Elements have their own nature. They do what they need to do—what they've been doing for millions and billions of years.

So, where do you come into all of this if the only thing that exists are laws, rules, and regulations that comprise the entire universe? What role do you play?

You do not play any role. You have no influence. Again, the entire universe consists of elements and laws. It plays by its own rules, no one else's. No single person is in charge of passing judgement. It is self-managing.

If you can understand this, you'll recognise the fruitlessness of obsessive searching and seeking. You honour the laws of the universe, stay away from these reactions and attachments, and live in complete freedom. This understanding of the truth—that no one other than yourself sets boundaries for you—is liberating.

Yet, you do need to be aware of one law. The law states you are free to do what you love, and you are free to create what you wish to enjoy your life. You can arrive at this complete freedom on your life's journey. You embody life, love, light, and spirituality.

Chapter 7

Attachment

Now that you recognise attachments, consider them and explore which might be a negative attachment and which might be a love attachment. Each is a side of the same coin. Observe where you feel attached to your negativity toward someone and where you've been attached through love. Then, work toward turning your negative attachments into positive ones. Once you begin to detach from negativity, you will hasten your personal growth.

When attached to a person or object, you try to absorb what you need from outside yourself. However, as you grow, you'll learn to develop what you need from the inside. After recognising what you want from the other person or object and why you are attached to it, you can spend your energy cultivating that quality within yourself.

For example, imagine being attached to someone because she is an athlete. You don't feel a sense of athleticism within you. You have that capacity—that energy—within you waiting to flourish, but you haven't given it an opportunity to grow. It's hard work to become an athlete. It is easier to form an attachment to someone with the skills and talents you desire.

Once you understand this concept, reflect on your life and notice your attachment. Each always offers an underlying message. Negative attachments are reflected through constantly bombarding someone, begging for physical, emotional, or mental contact. You're trying to absorb the energy from them in a negative way.

You can convert this to a positive attachment by releasing your cravings and obsession and patiently developing quiet love and respect while forming a healthy relationship. You're still attached, but not in a crazy way. This is how you bring your energy back within yourself and turn negative attachments into positive ones.

So, observe your attachments. Notice which attachments are positive and negative. What do you notice that is missing within yourself? How can you cultivate the qualities you see and desire in others for yourself? What can you do for yourself to bring your energy back into your being?

Recognising Emotions

Recognise your mental voice and the voice of your heart. The voice of your mind always chatters about doing more, wanting more, needing more. It is grandiose and wildly stokes your ego and imagination, telling you it is possible to conquer nature and the unknown. This mental voice tries to create that which is not there. It is solely concerned with fame and feeding the ego.

The voice of your heart is gentle. It's a whisper. It is slow and quietly speaks words of wisdom. It offers few words but always leads you in the right direction. It doesn't care about your ego. It doesn't care about how you're perceived in the world. It doesn't care about your personal problems and suffering.

The voice of the heart is the voice of the universe. The wisdom of the heart is the wisdom of the universe. It thinks for the universe, and its focus is the benefit of the universe. It does not think about you solely. There is no I in the voice of the heart. There's only us. It leads you to contribute to the health of all things in the universe.

It is essential to distinguish between the voice of the mind and the voice of the heart. The voice of the mind is not wrong. It's not bad, nor should it be totally neglected. But it needs to be in balance, alignment, and in conjunction with the voice of the heart. The mind's voice helps you care for your body in daily life. It supports your physical, mental, and emotional health. So, do not aspire to disregard the voice of the mind to revel solely in the voice of the heart and the universe. Both voices must work together.

Be observant. When the voice of the mind overtakes the voice of the heart, you begin to experience problems of the mind, emotions, and body. When you experience challenges with the mind, emotions, and body, it clearly indicates you are not in alignment with the universe. It is time to slow down and pay attention to the voice of the heart. This helps your life improve and contributes to the benefit of the universe.

The voice of the universe is the voice of service. It is how you serve another fellow human being with this unconditional love within your heart. Observe yourself. See if you align with your heart, and listen to it with a quiet mind so you can hear its pearls of wisdom.

Living in the Universe

Living in the universe, living from your heart, living from the source, and living from God. These are all different names for the bigger you. The universe is big; the mind is small but supports your body, emotions, and thoughts. It is up to you to determine how you like to live.

What part of your life is involved in cultivating the bigger side of you, and what part of your life is involved in remaining small? Observe how you communicate between the two. Do you combine them? If you try to separate yourself as either mind or heart, you will always experience conflict.

You begin to find peace once you realise that unconditional love is integral to the universe and you are not separate from it. You can see this connection clearly through emptying your mind, releasing your eagerness, and letting go of your needs and wants. When you do this, you will slowly merge into this unconditional love of the universe. Here, everything is available; everything is present. You begin to live from your heart.

Living from the heart is far more relaxing and beautiful than living a life concerned with the ego. The choice is yours. You can live a life of worry, stress, fear, and attachments of the mind and emotions. Or you can live from your heart, completely free, liberated, and connected to the universe.

Enlightenment Versus Transformation

Enlightenment happens when you first glimpse that you are not a limited being consisting solely of mind, body, and emotions. It is a recognition that you're bigger than this, more extravagant than this, that you are the universe itself.

You grew up with limited beliefs, thinking, and understanding that told you who you were and what you should do. Others told you, and then your mind began telling you, *This is what I want, this is what I need.* You built your life around this, securing yourself, protecting yourself, and collecting the things you felt would support and better your life. Suddenly, you have a new realisation. You understand that you are the universe. From one single glimpse—one single understanding and single experience—you become enlightened.

In contrast, transformation is a journey. It moves from the enlightened stage to becoming to completing your living self in the universe. In this transformation, you are living now from the bigger self of you, the universe of yourself. You experience the universe as the heart and as unconditional love. That is who you are in reality, and you live from this bigger you.

Listening to Your Heart Meditation

This meditation helps you overcome emotions and arrive at unconditional love. The ability to listen is valuable, and often we don't listen. We don't listen to ourselves. We don't listen to others. Internal dialogue fills our minds twenty-four-seven.

Yet, when you listen, your mind slows down. Listening intently opens your heart and slows your mind. The effect is profound. As soon as you listen well, your heart opens. It is instantaneous.

When you're thinking, you're mentally occupied, but when you're listening, you become more centred. All of your awareness comes in the middle of you. You become complete. So, how do you listen to yourself? This meditation will help you learn and practice listening to your heart.

Awaken to the Truth & Transform Your Emotions Into Unconditional Love

Find a comfortable position. You can sit on top of a cushion, on a blanket, on the floor, or in a chair. Sit up straight but remain relaxed. Release any tension you notice in your body. Let go of any thoughts, emotions, or sense of negativity you may be experiencing.

Relax your body and allow your body to begin to float. You feel light, like a feather, and carefree. Your mind and heart are widening.

Gently close your eyes and sense wherever you are. Feel a sense of expansion and oneness with the universe beyond your physical body. Take a couple of deep, slow breaths. Continue relaxing your body and bring that rhythm of yourself into harmony with the universe. Imagine you're breathing as the universe itself.

Release every worry you have. Extend those worries to the universe. The universe is intelligent. It can take care of everything. Allow yourself to feel a liberating sense of freedom now that you have no worries, cares, or responsibilities. You are as free as a kid. You're jumping for joy in your heart. Notice that feeling of love and freedom from everything. Spend some time experiencing this for a while.

Now that you're free, listen. Listen closely. Bring that listening into your heart. Bring your listening into the centre of your body, slightly towards your right, and hear the voice that's speaking from there.

It always has a message, and it's whispering to you. It's directing you to the path for you to take to live in peace and harmony so you can live a beautiful life. A life without stress or anxiety. Listen to your heart slowly, remaining aware of your heart and body. Take time to settle there for a while. Deepen your listening. Deepen into being yourself. Feel the peace of listening to your heart.

Spend as much time as you wish listening to your heart. Practice this for as long as you want, anywhere you like. Cultivate this capability to listen to your heart, connect with the universe, and live a life of unconditional love.

Entering Unconditional Love

How do you enter unconditional love? How do you connect with the ocean of love, the state of complete bliss? It requires faith.

Unconditional love is elusive if one has no faith or trust in oneself and the universe. However, the crucial and essential part of entering the state of bliss is having faith and trust that everything will be taken care of. All burdens are lifted from your shoulders. You no longer suffer under the weight of life, your past, future, nation, or the world and humanity. When you put complete faith in the universe, you know all will be cared for. You no longer worry every moment. Having faith and trust—building faith and trust—is essential for entering the state of bliss.

So, how do you find faith or build trust? You must realise you can deal with whatever arrives in front of you. You know worry, attachments, and stress do not solve problems. You see challenges clearly and realistically and know you can resolve them. When you've cultivated a pure heart and a pure mind, everything will go well, and you'll trust in yourself.

Trusting the universe is what slowly builds your faith every day. If you practice having faith in yourself and trust in yourself and the universe, it will welcome you in its arms. The universe works together with love, shares love, gives love, and generates love for you and everyone else around you.

Develop your trust and faith in the universe. When you do, you will embody a quality of self-confidence that allows you to deal with anything that comes your way. Building this faith and trust reduces your worry, attachment, and emotional volatility. You have a free heart. This free heart supports your expansion and opens the door to unconditional love and bliss.

Chapter 8

The Work

Life offers several spiritual paths. Sometimes, you may feel your path is harder than someone else's. But is this really true? That is the question.

For example, if you live in a family setting and desire to follow a spiritual path, you might look at a monk and feel like it would be much easier to live by yourself and dedicate your life to God. On the other hand, a monk may look at your family life and think it would be much easier to connect with God living in the middle of a family rather than living solo without any support.

Here's another example. If you live in a family setting, you might feel that someone who dedicated their life to being single, working hard, and attaining wealth, status, and freedom seems appealing. Yet that person may see your family life and long to have a family to lean on when times are tough and for a sense of community to come home to at night.

Further examples might be believing that the life of a musician, artist, athlete, astronaut, biologist, or any other option might be an easier path than yours. As humans, it is natural to look at someone else's path, feel ours is harder, and wish we'd chosen something else.

In this way, at one time or another, all of us look to other people and feel disheartened. But the thing is, regardless of which path you take, all humans must ascend the same levels of being. We all must face and overcome our bodily, mental, emotional, and life issues before we can dedicate ourselves to God.

So, if you feel disheartened and wish you had taken a different path, remember that everyone struggles.

I have sometimes struggled to move forward on my spiritual path while having a family. Yet, the family path is ideal for me, even if it isn't perfect. It is ideal because I have support, love, financial stability, and a home. It seems to help me address all levels of being. Being a family member has helped me feel well-supported, well-protected, and well-guarded in my spiritual journey.

On your spiritual journey, if you're thinking of moving out of the family path into being a working person or a monk, I suggest thinking twice and deeply contemplating where you are while recognising that everyone must transcend the same levels of being and overcome the same suffering. See where you find the most support, help, and love. Choose that path as your ideal path to reach God.

Being a Spiritual Explorer

Are you a spiritual explorer? What do I mean by this? First, consider if you are spiritual. Spirituality is found in all areas of life—teaching at schools, colleges, and universities, working in construction while erecting a building, or engineering and designing transportation. No matter who you are or what you do, recognise that spirituality is a deeper connection with ourselves. We use our body, mind, and emotions to go deeper. Our path is based on how we are inclined and trained, our past environments, and the encouragement we receive.

So first, consider where you're inclined to grow. Would you like to explore the mind, the body, emotions, lifestyle, or something else? Once you've done that, you'll dive deeper into your first choice and learn the foundational basics. It doesn't matter whether you choose medicine, dentistry, art, music, or parenthood; observe what you're drawn to. Learn and understand the fundamentals; once you understand them, you can move forward. You can go deeper and further. Continue moving forward as you understand the basis of it, its structure, and its creation as you apply your individuality to it.

Eventually, you'll discover you are a creator and no longer need to follow anyone else's work in your field. This is the ultimate state of creativity. You are continually creating new ideas and new forms. Now, at this point in your field, you access spirituality.

Let me explain. Spirituality, regardless of your field, augments creativity. Once your creativity reaches a high level, you begin to influence the creativity of others in your field. This level of creativity includes love, expansion, growth, movement, newness, and unlimited potential. Reaching this state within your field sets you on your spiritual journey.

From here onwards, your creativity and capabilities are endless. Your creativity produces beauty, which teaches and supports others. You've become a universal creator. Your creation is helping hundreds and hundreds of people as they explore and discover.

As you teach others, they explore and expand and begin teaching the people around them as well. The expansion continues, reaching further and further, helping other beings become beautiful. In this way, the deep exploration of your field leads to spiritual exploration and empowers you to uncover your unlimited potential.

Fear

We always seem to be fearful of something. We could be fearful of losing our job, losing a loved one, losing valuables, losing a great relationship, or losing anything that we accumulated over time. Fear, even though it's perceived as a negative thing, has some value.

It is common to hear, "Don't be afraid. Overcome your fear. Be brave. Stay positive. Everything will be fine." But those are false assumptions. They cause you to fool yourself.

Everything has its place, and everything has its reasons. Fear certainly has its place in our lives. But you need to understand what fear is and understand its role. But it is easier to discard fear or forget about it. We tend to delude ourselves because we don't want to go into fear. We want to run away from fear. But why is that?

It is because we don't yet know the usefulness of fear. Fear tells us we lack a certain capability within us. If you fear losing wealth, health, employment, or relationships, consider it carefully. Observe yourself, then ask, *Why am I fearful of losing money?* Is it because you don't know how to look after yourself if you don't have money? Perhaps you believe you're dependent on your spouse or other family members. In this way, the fear shows you an internal gap where you feel that if you didn't have someone to look after you, fear would rise up and take over your life.

Actually, fear is simply pointing out underdeveloped areas in life. In this example, it is saying, "You don't want to rely on someone else." It highlights your will to be fully equipped and completely safe within yourself. So, in a way, fear helps you grow. It helps you learn and expand.

Notice where in your life you have fear, then ask yourself what the fear is pointing out. Are you fearful of losing a loved one? Why? What don't you have within you that you're relying on that loved one for? Are they providing love, affection, and comfort? Can you provide that for yourself if that person is no longer there? Missing a loved one is okay. It's a natural process. But are you reliant? Are you going to be shattered? Are you going to be into pieces without that person? And if so, why?

Are you reliant on your job so much that it takes over your life, and you've surrendered yourself to it? Do you fear you wouldn't find another job, that you're incapable or strong enough to look elsewhere, or that your world would fall apart without that income stream? Observe your thoughts and learn from them. Let fear help make you stronger. Fear is not innately a bad thing. It helps you discover your faults. It helps you recognise and then fill gaps. Use fear to better yourself and evolve.

Pure Heart

A pure heart is when your heart is just yours. What does that mean? While growing up, you always gave your heart to somebody else. It could be your mother, father, aunt, uncle, siblings, an idol, or somebody you love the most. When you do that, that person is in your heart. That means you are not in your heart. When somebody else sits in your heart, the only love that you can give out or receive is from this person. It's similar to having a pure mind—as long as the thoughts of others are in your mind, you're not always able to see what you think.

In the same way, when your heart is pure, it is filled solely with your love. You are the origin and source of love without the influence of anyone else's feelings. Your feelings are original, your own. Your pure heart feels love for yourself and radiates that love outward, sharing this unconditional love with everyone else.

With this in mind, consider if you've ever had a pure heart. Since when have you had this pure heart? Most of us have never experienced a pure heart, as our hearts are often filled with other people rather than being pure.

This new awareness can be confusing. You may not recognise your own feelings. You may not know your own love. Take a moment to really sit with this idea and tune in to see if your heart is pure. Is the love you feel coming from your own internal source? Or is your love for yourself in existence because of someone else?

This new awareness of a pure heart allows you to release your attachments to others and empty your heart. It helps you step into pureness. When your heart is pure, unconditional love flows from your source—your heart—out toward everyone else.

Money and Consciousness When Helping Others

Often, we feel the best way to help others is through making money so we can share it. However, helping people financially is an indirect form of assistance. Financial assistance helps people externally and superficially—buying clothes, food, and shelter—whereas helping someone from within requires the development of consciousness.

To help someone financially, you must make money and offer it up charitably; sometimes, you may not even meet the people you help. This is a hands-off approach. The direct way of helping people is by helping them raise their consciousness to better help themselves. This helps in the true sense that somebody can improve and grow in their life.

A person is helpless not because he doesn't have money but because he doesn't know how to overcome his own distortions, blockages, and negative patterns. These traits are what prevent a person from looking after himself. Offering external help, such as money, only makes the individual poorer than he was already.

I once heard that if you give food to a hungry person, she'll always stay hungry. When a person is hungry, she's primed to learn. But when you offer food, she is momentarily satisfied and loses her hunger to grow and evolve.

Awaken to the Truth & Transform Your Emotions Into Unconditional Love

The best way to help someone is to teach them to raise their level of consciousness. Show her how to overcome the physical, mental, and emotional restrictions she's created for herself. That is a direct way of helping. This generosity is what changes lives.

The difference between money and consciousness arises from their constitution. Money is made of matter. Consciousness is formless and subtle. Money helps you purchase material things or services that support you to a certain level. Money can never directly help you raise your consciousness. Only consciousness raises consciousness because they belong to the same category.

Trying to use money to raise someone else's consciousness will not work. Money and consciousness operate on different planes. Think about this if your approach is to raise loads of money to expand your consciousness. It will not work. Money benefits many areas of life, especially bodies, which are in the material plane. You need to eat and be clothed and sheltered. This requires money.

But the rest of your development relies on consciousness. You can only expand your consciousness with the wisdom of consciousness. If you're drawn to help others, then raise your consciousness and offer support. A charitable donation of consciousness transforms lives far more than a financial donation.

Chapter 9

Trust and Faith

All of us have perceptions of God and what God represents. We've heard definitions and descriptions from religions, books, videos, and many sources about what God is. We have defined God ourselves through our imagination and vision. Some of us have experienced or interacted with spiritual figures, masters, or gurus who help us and support us in our journey as we get to know God. All of us have grown up with a notion of God.

Whether you consciously seek a relationship with God or unconsciously work toward it, it is a huge part of your life—all our lives. This oneness, this unity, this seeking and yearning is essential for humanity.

You cannot truly imagine God because your imagination and reality will inevitably differ. Only when you merge with God will you know its reality. You can't learn of God from someone else. Instead, the understanding of God comes from within you when you're ready. Ideas and beliefs do not matter because

God's reality completely differs from our learning, understanding and inquiring.

In my experience, when you practice and experience unconditional love, you step very close to knowing God. It is a total love you express towards all things that will lead you to experience God within you. Experiencing God within you merges you with God. You experience how it feels like to be God. This is what we all aspire to day in and day out. For every minute of our life, we desire this oneness with God and this beingness with God—to be God. This is your life's ultimate realisation.

The only path I can see toward merging with God is not dependent on being good or bad; it is about being kind and loving toward self and others.

Imagine having a singular dedication of love toward someone. You've focused your life on the other, and he or she calms you. You find contentment in your dedication to this loved one. Yet you're not free; you're focused. You're dedicated. You pray, meditate, and seek. But not until you become one with God does your external focus end. After you merge with God, everything dissolves in it.

Before then, you lived a normal life. The transformation between before-God-realisation and after-God-realisation is that you neglected or misunderstood many areas in your life. You were blinded because you were so singularly focused towards reaching your goal.

Once you reach it, you slowly begin to open to every other aspect of your life. You start to see where you lack understanding or talent and learn to improve. Then you start to live a basic, simple, complete life.

I share this from my personal experience. Your whole life was created to connect with God. I took about a year and a half to reach this God-realisation and transformation. Every cell of my body turned into completely new cells. The transformation process wasn't pleasant. It was an out-of-this-world experience, made more difficult by how long it took. A year and a half is a very long time to process such intensity of growth, expansion, and understanding in oneself, even as beautiful as it was. It was incredibly difficult to have the time, patience, perseverance, trust, and belief in myself to keep moving forward.

My advice to you? Go for it. Just go for it—100 per cent. Shed unimportant things in your life, focus entirely on what you seek, and give yourself 100 per cent to the process of transformation, understanding that with it comes responsibility. You'll feel peaceful, serene, calm, and tranquil when you come through the other side. If you can do this, it will change your life. I'll be here to support you if you need it.

Nothingness

What is nothingness, and how does it relate to God? When you're living your ordinary human life, there's something higher called God. Then, when you've attained God-realisation, there is nothing higher; there's only you—your God-self—and the truth. Everything is simple and basic.

Before God-realisation, you had needs. In your new God-realised life, you find abundance, everything you had wished for. Everything you've worked toward and felt passionate about is because you think it is outside yourself. But once you merge with God, you realise that nothing is bigger or better than that. Nothing exists beyond that. Everything else is simple; hence, you almost feel like there's nothing because you are everything. You are all that you are, the entire thing.

You have nothing left to chase, follow, or work towards when you are the entire thing. You're simply living and breathing and being free in a state of tranquillity.

Before merging with God, a person offers unconditional love to one thing, but once a person experiences God-realisation, it's as if God is forgotten. They've undergone such a transformation that the idea of God as separate from self no longer exists. If God and you merge and are no longer separate, your combined essence is everything. If you are everything, you become nothing;

even the word God dissolves. The only thing that remains is nothing.

Until you merge with God, this is difficult to understand. It seems odd to think that God existed before, and then God doesn't exist. However, this is simply about perspective. If you are still looking for God or envision God as sitting on a golden throne with a magic wand, you've not yet merged with God. Once you have a God-realisation, you'll no longer search for God but enter a space of simplicity and nothingness.

No Truth

When you become God-realised, you will see nothingness and simplicity. This also means you're in a state of no truth. You're living from a place of purity. You're not egotistical, pompous, or selfish. You're not walking around declaring, "I am God." Yet this space of no truth can be difficult to fathom and complicated to discuss with people who have not yet merged with God.

For example, imagine you desire to climb Mount Everest. All your life, you've been planning, working, and training towards climbing the highest mountain on earth. You're successful and reach the summit. Once you do that, you won't descend and say, "Now I'm ready to climb Mount Everest." Instead, that aspiration no longer exists for you. You've already achieved that goal. You climbed it and reached the top. You experienced everything you needed to experience. You're transformed.

Yet you won't say, "Mount Everest doesn't exist for me anymore." Achieving your life's goal has become a part of you. It feels normal now. It has become your reality. It no longer consumes your thoughts; it becomes nothing. Yet for climbers who have not yet summited, Mout Everest still exists.

The mountain exists for someone who has not ascended it. It no longer exists for the climbers who have summited. In this way, when you are God-realised, God no longer exists for you. God becomes a part of you and is everpresent as you live your normal, simple life.

When you are truly God-realised, you recognise the freedom, power, and unlimited potential before you. You need to be able to handle this, and you can only do that if you are truly merged with God and not faking or imagining it. Declaring that you have no one to answer to, are all-powerful, and can do anything you wish is a significant statement. You must have a level of integrity and responsibility when living a God-realised life, or you may misuse your new freedom. Maintain a sense of purity, and even though these beautiful attributes, skills, powers, and enormous potential are accessible, you'll remain neutral, uninterested, and detached. In essence, you see your new skills and just carry on living a simple life. That's the irony of it. When you graspingly reach for your goal, you may never attain it, yet when you attain it, you no longer desire it. You live in a place of no truth.

God Is Love, Love Is Freedom

It is easy to say God is love, and love is freedom. They work simultaneously. The desire you have to be one with God is the love you need to reach God-realisation, but once you merge and transform, you are suddenly free—free from desire for all things, including God. This is the beauty of it. Whether you're searching for freedom or searching for love, merging with God plays the most important part in everybody's life.

Yet amid the joy of the search is a fear of losing one's identity. There's a fear of having unlimited potential and a fear of nothingness. The combination of these fears prevents us from actualising God-realisation. Yet the truth is there is nothing to be afraid of.

Do not be afraid of becoming nothing, losing love, not having God in your life, being suspended in emptiness or of the process of transformation itself. You will come through the other side. It's okay not to know in advance how you'll cope with it. It's okay not yet to know what your life will look like. And it's okay that everything as you know it will change.

Your love will increase more than your fear. Your unconditional love—for yourself and others—will help you arrive at God. Unconditional love and acceptance of this unconditional love towards God are required to merge with God. Trust. Allow yourself to believe everything will be taken care of, and simply devote yourself to God. This attention, focus, dedication, and devotion will get you through to the other side, without a doubt.

Nothingness and Allness

Let's take a moment to clarify the misconception between nothingness and allness. After your God-realisation, you experience everything as you and everything as all that is. So where is this nothingness? How can you have allness and nothingness?

Allness is experienced in your being, heart, soul, and every cell of your body, but nothingness is experienced in your mind.

Nothingness is the result of allness in everything. Your mind is empty. It has nothing to conquer. It has no wants or needs. It is totally empty in the sense that it is not chasing anything. It's not after anything. There's nothing to focus on to achieve anything. That's where the nothingness comes from. Nothingness doesn't mean you don't exist, or you don't have a life, or you're dead, or any of those kinds of concepts. It's just the experience of itself—the mind. The mind is in a state of nothingness without needs, cravings, attachments, or desires. You are full.

Think about this again: nothingness is experienced in the mind, whereas allness is experienced in your being. The mind in the state of nothingness says there is emptiness. But the Being in allness sees itself as everything. How you explain your state depends on your point of view. They both equally exist. One is in the mind, and one is in the heart, soul, and body.

Beauty comes from balancing allness and nothingness and appreciating both. Be satisfied with both. This uniqueness of experiencing both at once is the beauty of fulfilment, contentment, peace, and completion.

Giving Everything

Giving everything means you're allowing yourself to give your all. For example, if you've been running toward love, you're giving all your love and focusing it on one thing. You're taking your love from everything else and focusing it on one object. You empty yourself completely to this love.

Similarly, when you choose to love God and pull love from all your peripheral attachments, focusing it on God, you open up to God itself. The unlimited potential of love flows right back through to you. When you've given up everything, you transform and merge with God, and then everything flows back to you, and you get to keep it.

This is how it has worked for me in all areas of life. Whether it is the body, mind, emotions, love, life,

133

spirituality, money, whatever it is, that area of life that you run away from, feel negative towards, or feel you lack or fear, give everything to it. Don't keep anything to yourself. Surrender yourself and give all of it to it.

Then, you will discover limitlessness. This realisation is crucial because this process happens in all areas of your life. By learning this and understanding it, you will see that everything is connected to the unlimitedness of every area of life. We try to hold onto something or are fearful of something because we feel there isn't enough of it. When you tightly hold onto something, you are constricted. But when you begin to let go of the thing you were grasping, everything opens up. You see and connect with the breadth of all areas of life, and you eventually become your complete self—unlimited in everything.

External Source

We tend to surround ourselves with particular people, places, or environments. We travel abroad, go shopping, have a nice meal, go for walks, meet our friends, and go to parties. Essentially, we use external environments to create certain feelings, vibrations, and frequencies. We artificially create situations to make up for what we don't have within us.

However, walking in nature is different. Flowers, plants, water, and earth are not artificially created. We have not created the atmosphere but choose to engage with it.

So there are two things: we create a certain atmosphere around us that we think is good and pleasant, and alternatively, we take ourselves into natural environments because we feel relaxed, calm, and serene there. They both are pretty much the same because you're looking for stimulus from outside yourself in each instance.

As you grow, you aspire to create the atmosphere you desire within yourself. Anything you try to create outside can only please your senses because your senses are outwardly facing. What you're trying to do is calm your senses. You want to relax, slow down, and ease your senses. This only happens inside of us.

Turning inward requires effort. The effort you put into external experiences now needs to be pulled inward. These experiences need to originate from inside you—you need to find what is within you that pleases you and supports your growth.

You cannot surround yourself with beautiful people and expect to turn beautiful. Yet that is often what we try to do. Surrounding yourself with beauty to feel beautiful is only temporary, and it needs to be continuously maintained and requires immense time and energy. Yes, experiencing external beauty is nice; we don't need to cut that out of life completely. But most of your efforts to find and attain beauty must arise from inside you.

So, what does it mean to grow internally and find beauty from the inside out? Beauty is something that we cannot superficially create. We cannot be around beautiful people and become beautiful. We can only adapt, copy, and reflect. We have not originated beauty from within. Beauty is something you find only when going deeply into yourself. You must search the hidden corners of your heart and soul to find beautiful places. Then, cultivate your beauty from that point by exploring your inner self further. As you develop your inner beauty, you expand it by bringing your unique self into the world, manifesting and sharing your beauty.

The same is true for love. Just because you're surrounded by loving people doesn't mean you are loving. It doesn't work that way. You need to find the love inside of you, then bring that love outside of you and share it with people. You must find the love inside yourself rather than rely on love from external sources.

You must be vigilant, awake, and aware to spot when you rely on external sources versus internal sources. Everything you see outside you is already inside you because you're looking at reflections. Those reflections teach you that what you see exists within you. So, find that place within you. Rather than focus on creating a peaceful external environment, find that place of peace inside of you and bring it out for yourself and to share with others.

Awaken to the Truth & Transform Your Emotions Into Unconditional Love

You'll begin to rely less on external sources and environments and find everything from within. Once you find what you need, cultivate it, expand it, and share it with others. And this leads to true beauty, true love, and true peace.

Chapter 10

Unconditional Love

What is the difference between love and unconditional love? When you focus your love energy towards one particular thing or a person, you may become attached. The attachment can become obsessive and turn ugly.

With unconditional love, you overcome this singular focus. You move beyond the obsession. You harmonise and blend with your object of love. You become one with it. It's almost like an eclipse.

When two things that love each other become one, they eclipse each other. The individuality of each disappears, resulting in an explosion of unconditional love. Unconditional love has no obsessive focus—no heightened concentration. Instead, unconditional love offers three-hundred-sixty degrees of love, an expansion of love all around you.

We all aspire to reach this feeling of wholeness and beauty that comes from unconditional love.

If you'd like to learn more about this process, please explore my online course, *Transform Your Emotions Into Unconditional Love,* https://bit.ly/3QjsJ28.

Discipline of the Heart

What is discipline of the heart? It's how we manage our feelings. When we're unaware of our feelings, we may become attached to or love different things. Yet, we don't understand the consequences of this attachment.

If you're not used to using your feelings, and you're careless about them, attaching them to various external objects, the consequence is accumulating many feelings without the ability to distinguish between each. Nor will you have the discipline to deal with your feelings individually. This creates a confusion of feelings. So, be careful when you send your feelings to someone or something.

It is about becoming aware of your feelings. It is good to become aware of your feelings. Sit with them and notice how your emotions interact with each other, especially around the things or people you love. Observe your feelings and how they manifest toward the person or the thing you love.

Disciplining your feelings means moving on without pulling all the past feelings into the present moment. This discipline helps you to move on and detach from the emotions of the past. Observe yourself in everyday moments, and notice how your past feelings come into the present day. Do these feelings keep you haunted and repeating the same actions? Use this reflection as an opportunity to restrict and separate them to identify each better.

Gaining knowledge about your feelings and noticing how they perform is the discipline you will develop. If you have too many feelings, it may feel overwhelming to observe them. Take your time and react to your feelings slowly. Take each, one by one, and become aware of them. Be in the present moment with them and discard what no longer serves you. Identifying your past feelings and your present feelings helps you reduce overwhelm. In this way, you slowly become aware of emotions that support and uplift you, and you begin to live a more emotionally disciplined life.

Loving Everything

If you're the kind of person who grew up loving everything and wanting to experience everything, life is like being a kid in a candy store. But you don't realise that when you're a kid. When you are young, you're unconscious of your feelings and believe you can love everything. The moment you say you love something, you're attached to that. This attachment is subtle but pervasive.

As an adult, you're more conscious of your feelings and need to become aware of your attachments. Observe what you feel and think when considering the people and objects you love. Can you live your life without constantly mentioning how much you love someone or something? Is it possible to go even an hour without expressing your love for something?

Imagine your life; perhaps you go shopping, go to clubs, go to restaurants, go to parties, and visit with friends, family, and other relatives. Imagine the amount of feelings you accumulate through these activities. What happens with those feelings? Most likely, you're unaware of all the attachments that go with your feelings. As you engage with the world, it is as if a thousand strings connect from your heart to your object of attachment, and you're likely not even aware of it.

However, as you observe yourself, notice your attachments, and then release them, you move closer to unconditional love. A love that is strong but not attached. Unconditional love offers complete freedom and bliss. The glory of non-attachment is even greater than the love we feel with multiple individual attachments.

When you're unconscious, you try to love the entire earth and all the people, yet it is still one by one; it's never 360 degrees. Unconditional love is one love of 360 degrees. It is a total, complete love rather than being divided individually and multiplied. Aspire to live in a state of unconditional love without attachment to any individual objects or things. See if you abstain from expressing your love for any one object.

Every time you see something beautiful. Every time you see something amazing. See if you can go past it. See it as equal to everything else. When you can, you have reached true love, where you see everything as one and the same without attachment to anything.

Open Heart

What is an open heart? An open heart is free. It's pure. It has no restrictions. It has no choice. It is not bound. It's open, which means anything and anyone can come in. Anything and anyone can flow out of it. You don't hold on to anything. You're not attached.

You see something. You experience it. You feel the joy of it. And if that something wants to go, you release it without regrets. There's no pain. There's no suffering as the thing comes and goes; you remain the same.

This is an open heart, the pure heart which is always loving, nurturing, giving, receiving, and comforting. Pure and simple. No choosing.

All of us can develop this open heart, which is a mature heart, a mother's heart, always open, welcoming, and pure in nature.

What Is Meditation

Meditation is a process of learning to be aware of ourselves in a set condition. Through meditation, you learn to recognise your thoughts, emotions, and body. Meditation can be done anywhere that you can focus.

Here are a few steps to help you meditate. First, find a quiet space where you will not be disturbed and are free from distractions. Turn your phone to silent.

Second, sit in a comfortable position. You can sit on top of a cushion, on a blanket, on the floor, or in a chair. Sit up straight but remain relaxed. Release any tension you notice in your body.

Third, breathe gently, inhaling and exhaling naturally.

Fourth, let distractions come and go. If your mind wanders, acknowledge the thought that has distracted you, but do not dwell on it. Then, gently bring your attention back to your breath and stay awake. Distraction during meditation is inevitable and is a concern for many, but know it is okay and natural. You're simply letting thoughts and emotions rise and fall.

Meditating in this way for five to ten minutes daily is a significant achievement. Some people like to meditate longer, but that comes only through practice. The important thing with meditation is consistency. Do it every day, and you'll gently and step by step build your awareness.

Mind to the Heart

When you first begin to meditate, you think, imagine, and envision everything is in the mind. Imagine the mind as a small version of the universe—a smaller circle or a smaller sphere inside the big sphere. This small sphere is the mind you use every day. You process this huge universe through your little mind, trying to understand your small experiences. You build your daily activities on your understanding of your smaller life. Rarely does anyone have a huge experience, and when we do, our minds contract because we can't understand it; it's too overwhelming.

Yet your goal is to wake up to this bigger life of the universe. You must emerge from the smaller mind. How do you do this? The smaller mind is filled with ideas and knowledge of the past—concepts you think and imagine are right. What you see around you is accumulated in your smaller mind. This is an important part of your mind's development. But the next step is the leap from the smaller mind to the universe.

This can feel challenging at first, so it is important to remember to keep moving forward even when you feel overwhelmed. As you move through your life journey while using your little mind, it is easy to get stuck and attached to all kinds of experiences. These experiences may be bodily, emotional, mental, relationships or anything else. Attachment to these experiences causes you to stick to a certain area and spend years in that experience. But as you deepen your self-awareness, you can begin moving forward, which helps you begin to glimpse the universal itself.

The universe is basically the heart—your heart. Connecting with your heart is the next step after understanding your mind. Connecting with your heart leads to your connection with the universe. Once you reach the universe through your heart, you begin to understand, embody, and express unconditional love.

To do this, allow all your life experiences to flow through you. Keep your mind open and embrace everything while remaining detached. Always move forward. Allow your mind to remain empty and unblocked, and then you will arrive at your heart, where you can begin to express unconditional love. From this unconditionally loving heart, you have access to the universe.

Quantum Jump Guided Meditation

Welcome to quantum jump, guided meditation. If you'd like, arrange some flowers, light a candle, or burn incense to create a serene atmosphere. Find a comfortable position sitting on a cushion, on a blanket, on the floor, or in a chair. Sit up straight but remain relaxed. Gently close your eyes and take a couple of deep, slow breaths in and out. Release any tension you notice in your body.

Awaken to the Truth & Transform Your Emotions Into Unconditional Love

Relax and allow your mind to flow and your emotions to be just whatever they are. Simply relax and let go.

Free yourself from all thinking or holding on to things, and allow yourself to melt and dissolve into wherever you are. Try to embody a sense of nothingness.

Imagine letting go. You may feel this means letting go of one thought or a couple of thoughts. One idea, one attachment, or multiple attachments. Maybe releasing a few concepts. But that is barely letting go.

Letting go means taking a quantum jump. To do this, you let go of your worries about yourself. You may worry about your body, your work, your family, your health, and your friends, or you may worry about what might happen tomorrow or in the future.

This meditation helps you let go of all that. You'll release almost everything. You'll leave it behind. You'll discard everything you have on your hands and place your worries into the ocean of love. This ocean of love takes care of everything.

You can leave everything—all your problems, worries, responsibilities, thoughts, and ideas. It's as though you're leaving everything behind. Just jumping off the cliff.

You close your eyes, not knowing where you're jumping into. You completely remove yourself from wherever you are right now. But you're not irresponsibly leaving your worries behind. You're being responsible by placing your worries, your problems, your issues, everything, into the hands of the universe.

The ocean of love is something bigger than you. It's more intelligent than you. It is also a part of you that you haven't recognised yet.

The moment you leave these worries and responsibilities into the hands of this ocean—your bigger self—you become totally free. This freedom, which is the beauty, love, and newness that you encounter when the ocean of love, is taking care of all your problems. You trust that by believing in yourself and believing in your connection and love for the universe, everything will be okay. The bigger intelligence takes care of you. It frees you of your responsibilities, and you can let go.

Now, stay in this freedom that you feel after jumping off the cliff and releasing your worries and responsibilities to the ocean of love. Stay in this freeness for the next five minutes.

As you begin to shift out of this meditation, continue to stay in this freeness. Enjoy the freedom of responsibilities. Enjoy being you. Practice this meditation once or twice a day. Let go of all your worries and enjoy this freedom of being who you are.

Now, gently move your arms, legs, and shoulders. Bring the awareness back into your body. Gently open your eyes and recognise where you are. Take a couple of deep, slow breaths. You have now completed quantum jump guided meditation. Move into your beautiful day.

Living from Your Heart

What does it mean to live from your heart? Living from your heart is a bit difficult to describe because you still have to use a little bit of your mind to explain this. Living from your heart feels like being at home, centred, comfortable, able to breathe easily, relaxed and not worried. You're not overthinking or fearful. You feel wholesome, empty, present, not pulled by anything or attracted to anything but admiring everything. You see everything and are present with everything in a stable, pleasant, loving way.

You're living from within you. You're not living with any ideas. You're not living with outside pressure or inside expectations. You're just living the best way you can live right now with all the possibilities available to you. You're not working towards anything. Instead, you're living with what you have—good or bad, right or wrong. You are in this situation; you are in this place. You are living from here. That's all there is to it.

Where will you go from here? What will happen? These thoughts still come. But mostly, you're living in a state of peace. As long as you have your mind, you will still have its functions and its thoughts, which will take a long time to eradicate. Clearing the mind is a long process. But once you overcome your negative thinking, negative emotions, and fearfulness, you begin to live in your heart and from your heart.

149

Life becomes beautiful and simple. It is humbling. You have nothing to worry about. Looking back, you wonder why you spent so much time imagining things. This concept is not new. It's not that you have never lived from your heart. You have lived from your heart many moments in your life. But we don't recognise it because it's not that often. Yet, you rarely recognise it when you do. Very quickly, you move into your mind because that is what occupies so much of your life.

Daily, you rely on your mind. It's only natural. You have many responsibilities and things that must be done. You very rarely get to stay in your heart and live from there. But when you can, it is stabilising.

You have already lived in your heart in those happy moments where you felt free or celebrated. You might have had many such occasions. But the aspiration is to live from your heart for most of your day, most of your week, and as often as possible. With practice, eventually, it will become the norm.

How much life is lived from the heart varies from person to person. The more relaxed and peaceful you are, the easier it will be to stay there longer. It is a simple thing, but not always easy to do. Living from your heart is a beautiful, simple, and humble way to move through life.

Awareness of the Mind

What happens to awareness when you live from your heart? Awareness is a quality of the mind. It is a higher quality of the mind than thinking because, in thinking, you connect many thoughts, leading to results, ideas, outcomes, or actions. In contrast, awareness is a quiet state of mind used to understand your thoughts and mental behaviours.

When you move into the heart, you'll use awareness less because you're in tune with unconditional love, which is the openness of the heart. Unconditional love is free of comparison. Imagine a flower bud. It is compact, focused, tight, intense, and not free. But then the flower blossoms, opening its petals to the sun and sharing its fragrance with the world. Its beauty is like unconditional love. The blossom has no attachment to one person, saving all its fragrance just for them. The flower has no singular focus; it shares its beauty with everyone. This is the difference between love and unconditional love.

When you say you love somebody, you're concentrated; your focus is singular. When you express unconditional love, you're being like the flower. You're opening yourself to everyone and everything. You have a constant feeling of love for all without a need to focus it. Unconditional love is subtle rather than extravagant. You don't feel like you're on top of the world, yet you feel peacefully grounded. You're not looking for anything or wanting anything because you have everything you need.

In typical daily life, you always want something. You want to feel comforted, energised, buzzy, affectionate, joyful. This desire to experience a feeling comes from attachments and singular focus. Whereas with an open, pure heart, unconditional love offers a constant presence of peaceful love. It is subtle and soft. You no longer need to look for anything else when you have that feeling.

In this way, awareness differs from living from the heart and unconditional love. It is a subtle and beautiful state to be in.

The Universal Heart

When you live from your heart, you begin to develop a universal heart. When you enter this state, you feel you don't need anything. This is because everything exists in this universal heart.

You no longer fear that anything will be taken from you. For example, imagine living in a house filled with food, drink, luxury, and everything you wish for. Would you live in fear and begin stealing from the house, hoarding goods elsewhere? The house has everything you need. It's already here. It's crystal clear. It's as clear as a tree next to you. A plant next to you. You can see everything existing in one plane, so you don't need to save anything.

You don't need to safeguard, collect, steal, or store anything. All you need is right in front of you.

You use what you use. And you leave the rest. This is the reality of universal love. When you're not living in universal love, you feel you don't have enough, and your mind tells you you're limited. But when you're living from your unconditional heart, you have the entire universe as the source and resource for whatever you wish to create, use, experience, and live. When you live in your universal heart, you no longer need to accumulate anything; everything exists in this loving reality.

Falling Into Your Heart

When you enter the universal heart, it is like falling into the heart from the mind. It's as though you've been dropped down from the head into the heart. It's a freefall, a quantum leap. It's a skydive, and you don't know where you will land. It requires trust. It demands self-confidence. Moving from the mind to the heart can be scary. You feel like you're falling through darkness, and you don't know where you'll land. That is what you're afraid of.

Everybody can discover their universal heart. But is everyone willing to let go? Are you willing to jump without support, a rope to hold on to, and without knowing where you'll land? Do you dare? Does letting go of everything you can think of hold you back?

You fear the unknown, but you have the capacity to develop courage, strength, and self-trust to make that quantum leap. Compose yourself. Believe in yourself. You will survive no matter what happens. You are stronger than you think you are.

When you reach that point in life where nothing shakes you anymore, regardless of what happens, you have the capacity to transform your life. At that moment, you've gathered the courage to fall into your heart. When you do this, you will look back and see this was the right decision at the perfect time.

Unlimited Potential

What is unlimited potential? What does eternity mean? It means endlessness. You experience a continuous process of constant creation. You're self-reliant, the source of everything. You can create as many things as you wish with this unlimited potential. You have access to never-ending newness because creation is newness, and you are creating every moment. Something is being created.

In that sense, when you open up to your unlimited potential, you feel that you can create an endless number of things—ideas, visions, manifestation—all of it expands outward with no end in sight.

You have this unlimited source inside of you that you can use to create anything you like in any field in any direction you like. You have been doing this all your life.

Awaken to the Truth & Transform Your Emotions
Into Unconditional Love

It's not something new. You've known its presence all along, but you just didn't know how to express this unlimited potential.

Imagine you are a painter, an artist. You spend most of your time working nine to five, even though you have a little artistic passion somewhere in you. Your artistry expresses itself sometimes, but mainly, you end up staying busy with your everyday life and not pursuing your passion. But your artistic unlimited potential is still there, unexplored. Or you've dabbled some but not enough to where it becomes a continuous flow of newness. This continuous flow of newness gives meaning to life and leads to contentment, creativity, satisfaction, and a sense of eternity. The unlimited potential in you gives you a beautiful sense of never-ending life. It is a beautiful experience to have.

You're not reliant on anyone else. You are your own creative source, creating things that have never been seen before. You are connected to the universe and in flow. You can access the source, which supports all aspects of your life. You are now the person you've always searched for.

We all have this capacity; we just have to discover and connect with it. Where is this newness, this creativity in you? Is it flowing? Have you yet to discover this for yourself? If so, simply look within. Observe your life and use what you learn to grow. Unlimited potential is waiting for you. All you need to do is look around, discover it, and say yes to it.

Being of Service

You've been handed unlimited potential and the key to an eternal life of creativity and newness. With this new potential, your responsibility is to serve people and uplift humanity. Everybody has been given this key, but not everyone uses it to unlock their unlimited potential and use the waiting talents and gifts.

Each of us has been uniquely designed to express newness and creativity and use this manifestation to help humanity raise consciousness. This is what service means—serving humanity by authentically helping each other using your unique gifts and creations. Being of service means helping others transform their lives.

You make use of the original material meant for you. You create, and then you share. This original material transformed through you helps you get where you need to go, and once you've gotten there, you can serve others.

You can still be of service without unlocking your unlimited potential, but it will be a longer, slower, and more difficult process. But with the purity of unlimited potential supporting your creation, you can effectively and effortlessly help others.

When connecting with unlimited potential, the original material you access is a million times stronger, better, and more effective. So, in this way, you can see how you have been created to transform things for the betterment of humanity. The best thing for humanity is for each of us to take advantage of this potential. We all must discover this creativity within, discover our innate talents, and bring them out to share. This has to be our life's primary goal rather than a hobby or something we attend to in our spare time. We must each realise our authentic gifts, turn them into reality, and be of service.

The Heart Speaks

Is it hard to believe that the heart actually speaks? The heart speaks very slowly, very quietly, without any movement. It speaks like an old woman—very wise and to the point. It offers no confusion. It offers no commands. It simply says what it means without negotiation, discussion, or arguments. It simply speaks.

It speaks several times. You'll hear it if you're open to listening. You must be able to listen deeply and develop a capacity to hear because the heart speaks softly, quietly and slowly.

Over the years, you've gotten used to listening to your mind, which is loud, active, and fast. You may have forgotten the voice of the heart even exists. The first step in listening to the heart is to practice quieting the mind. The simple act of quieting the mind helps you feel calmer and more relaxed. Yet the true purpose of quieting the mind is so you can listen to your heart.

The heart, being the master of the universe, has profound wisdom and kindness in its words. Hearing the heart is a beautiful experience. You can hear it in your body, in your soul, and all around you. Its words are precious, and each person's heart speaks directly to them. We all hear different things.

It is up to you to learn how to listen to your heart. You can spend a whole day listening to your heart, and it will be time well spent. Each time it speaks, it has something new to say. It never repeats itself. Take the time to quiet your mind through meditation so you can listen deeply to the precious voice of your heart.

How to Speak from Your Heart

Speaking from the heart means that your words do not arise from thought. When your heart connects to your voice, its words come directly from your mouth. You no longer let your mind and thoughts manage your voice. Instead, the wisdom of your heart comes to the surface. And whatever you speak are pearls of wisdom.

Learning to speak from your heart requires a process. It does not happen overnight. The process begins in the body. You learn to discipline the body and bring it to optimal health. Then, you teach the body to listen to the mind, and the mind uses the body's assistance. The body begins to listen to the mind. With support from the body, the mind develops and expands its knowledge. It develops awareness, the mind's highest quality.

After awareness, the mind moves into the realm of light. Once it achieves this point, the mind is purified. When the mind is purified, it becomes quieter and has gained the capacity to be settled, calm, and can listen. The mind has learned it's okay to remain silent.

Once the mind has arrived at this point, awareness drops down to the heart. The heart's functions are assessed, and once the heart is purified, all emotions are overcome, and attachments are left behind. Your heart is now free to experience the vastness of unconditional love. Unconditional love is used daily to provide service and help to humanity.

This is the way to open and master your heart. When the heart arrives at this point, it starts to speak and share its wisdom. The wisdom of the heart—which is the origin of creation—is expressed through your mouth as pearls of wisdom. You share the original words of truth. It feels as if it is coming from nowhere, yet those words are originated in your heart and shared thanks to your efforts.

Follow Your Heart

Following your heart means you know who you are. You've been in contact with your heart. You've been passionate, kind, and loving from a very young age. You have been communicating with your heart and speaking its truth for a very long time. Have you followed your heart through your life, through thick and thin, sorrow and pain, whether rich or poor? Have you made it this far because you believed in your heart and believed in yourself?

Following your heart was fraught with challenges. You faced all your problems, whatever they were. But you did it. You went through it. You stood by yourself. You expanded through the experience. Now, you see the fruit of your hard work. Following your heart means you have stayed by your heart throughout your life.

Do you know love? Have you been connected to universal love? Once you connect with universal love, you'll remain there. If you haven't followed your heart and have been tempted by worldly pleasures, desires, and worldly, flashy things, you've strayed away from your heart.

It is not too late to pick up your heart where you left off. Once again, develop your connection with yourself with the universe. Be authentically you. This is bravery. Have the courage to face whatever might come when following your heart. If you have that and are ready to face that, then you can easily follow your heart. The question is, are you ready to take that step? No one can answer it but you.

Open Your Heart Meditation

In this meditation, to open your heart, take a prayer position that suits you. It may be sitting with your palms together or lying down with your palms facing up. You can use a candle in a darker room for a warm light. Burn incense if you wish. You can also play music in the background if it helps you relax.

Take a few deep, slow breaths, and allow your body, mind, and emotions to slow down naturally. Once you feel relaxed, bring your awareness into your heart area.

Send love towards anyone you deeply care for. If you bring to mind someone that triggers a reaction within you, bring your love towards this feeling. Now send this love to either the person you love or to any of the feelings that are coming up within you.

Continue sending love as long as you feel you're harmonizing with the energies of the person you love or with the feelings of worry, anger, or resentment. After sending your love to this person or these emotions, you will naturally feel a sense of harmony with the person or emotions if you've not hidden behind your feelings.

Now is the time to express your gratitude. If you are feeling responsible for past errors, accept your mistakes and end this meditation with love. In this way, when you sit in the meditation of love, you send love energy towards the object, person, or feeling and wait until this love melts and expands into unconditional love.

This meditation can be done anywhere at any time. It doesn't necessarily have to be done in a set place. This heals and clears your heart of past or present situations and emotions.

Acknowledgements

I would like to thank my family, friends, and other spiritual and non-spiritual members of my life who have directly or indirectly contributed to this book and made this journey possible.

About Smitha

Smitha Jagadish has loved the written word since she was a little girl, always using a diary or journal to express herself. She often jokes, "Even though I was raised in India and knew very little English, I've now written two books in English"! She resides in beautiful England with her hubby, two children, and a pet dog.

Smitha Jagadish writes spiritual books about meditation, awakening, wisdom teachings, self-discovery, and how to work with the universe. She is a spiritual teacher who offers training courses that help new seekers navigate the tricky waters of self-discovery. She also offers a training program for spiritual coaches. Learn more at www.theschoolforenlightenment.com.

A Favor to Ask

Thank you for taking the time to read this book.

I hope you found it thought-provoking and inspiring.

I'd love to hear your feedback,
so please head over to Amazon or wherever you
purchased this book to leave an honest review.
Every review matters, and your responses help me
make future books better.

I thank you endlessly.

Printed in Great Britain
by Amazon

32489575R00097